The Esperanza Cook Book

Louise Johnson

Maple Lane Publishing - Surrey, British Columbia

The Esperanza Cook Book.

Cover Design by Chris Kielesinski
Layout, design and production
by Phil Hood and Bill Glasgow of Mediaworks Inc.

ISBN 0-921966-008

Printed in Canada

THE WEST COAST of Vancouver Island is called the Graveyard of the Pacific. The rugged coastline has rock face mountains descending into the depths of the sea. Shallow water and jagged rocks make navigation treacherous. Sudden winds and off-sea storms disturb the water continuously. Seldom are there calm and peaceful seas.

The community of Esperanza is 100 miles northwest of Campbell River on the inside passage between Nootka Island and the mainland of Vancouver Island.

The Rugged Coast
of
Vancouver Island

This Book is Dedicated in Memory of
The Esperanza General Hospital (1937-1973)

To those who have fed, comforted and nourished
The sick, the lonely, the strangers

and to the Many Family and Friends of
Vancouver Island's isolated West Coast
Throughout Nootka Mission's History

Acknowledgement

This cook book could not have been compiled
without the assistance of many people.

I am deeply grateful to each one.

Special Thanks to

- Those who submitted such delightful recipies

- Jean Hood who typed every recipe

- Dell Johnson for proof reading.

- Bill Glasgow for the computer typesetting

and to the distinguished artists

Chris Kielesinski for the cover and cartoons

Rick Charles for the Sketches of Esperanza.

Contents

Breads

Whole Wheat Pancakes

from Colleen Shonwise, Tahsis, B.C.

Makes 12

Ingredients:
- 1/3 cup whole wheat flour
- 1 cup white flour
- 1 Tsp. sugar
- 3 Tsp. baking powder
- 1/2 Tsp. salt
- 1/4 cup cornmeal (optional)
- 1/2 cup oil
- 2 beaten eggs
- 1 1/2 cups milk

Method:

Place in a bowl, mix well. Pour on hot greased griddle or frying pan. Cook until bubbles are popping. Flip over and cook second side for approximately same time.

Best Cornmeal Bread

from Laura Brisbane, Bellingham, Wash.

Temperature is 400°F
Baking time is 25 minutes
Uses an 8 inch pan, buttered

Ingredients:
- 1 cup cornmeal
- 1 cup flour
- 4 Tbsp. sugar
- 1 Tbsp. baking powder
- 1 Tsp. salt
- 1/3 cup oil
- 1 egg
- 1 cup milk

Method:

Combine dry ingredients and mix well. Beat egg and milk together, add oil. Mix until just blended. Bake.

Nana's Potato Bread

from Anna Glasgow, Abbotsford, B.C.

Uses a large griddle

Ingredients:
- 6 large potatoes
- 1 cup process cheese spread
- 2 cups of flour
- 1 cup milk
- pinch of salt

Method:
Boil and mash the potatoes. Add cheese, flour, milk, and the pinch of salt. Roll out the dough on a floured table to between 1/8 inch and 1/4 inch thick. Cut 3"-4" squares and cook on griddle for 10 minutes (until golden brown)

Wheaten Bread

from Mames McPherson, Toronto, Ont.

Temperature is 375°
Baking time is 60 minutes
Uses an 8 inch square pan, buttered

Ingredients:
- 1 1/2 cups white flour
- 2 Tsp. soda
- 1 Tsp. salt
- 1/4 cup sugar
- 3 cups whole wheat flour
- 2 cups buttermilk

Method:
Sift flour, soda, salt, sugar and whole wheat flour together. Blend in buttermilk. Roll in a ball. Place in pan. Cut an "X" on top of it. Bake. Cool on rack. (You can substitute milk powder, wheat germ, bran in place of the whole wheat flour.) Eat warm.

Dinner Buns

from Barbara Haskell, Three Hills, Alberta

Makes 50 - 60 buns
Temperature is 350°
Baking time is 15 minutes

Ingredients:
- 2 eggs
- 1 Tsp. salt
- 2/3 cup sugar
- 4 cups warm water
- 2 Tbsp. dry yeast
- 3 Tbsp. oil
- 10 cups flour

Method:
Stir eggs in large bow. Add salt, sugar and warm water. Stir well. Sprinkle with yeast. Let sit for 12 minutes. Then add oil and flour. Add a little more flour till it feels right. (It will be quite sticky.) Knead for 5 minutes. After you have added all the flour grease bowl and cover dough with saran wrap. Cover with a tea towel. Let rise till double. Shape into buns and let rise again till double. Bake.

Cold Water Buns

from Esperanza Kitchen

Makes 100 buns
Temperature is 350°

Ingredients:
- 6 cups water
- 2 Tbsp. yeast
- 1 or 2 Tsp. sugar
- 1 Tbsp. salt
- 2 cups flour
- 1 cup oil
- 1/2 cup sugar
- 2 - 3 beaten eggs
- 16 cups flour

Method:
At 12 Noon combine 6 cups cold water, yeast, 1 or 2 Tbsp. sugar and 2 cups flour. Do not stir. At 2 o'clock add oil, 1/2 cup sugar, 1 Tbsp. salt, eggs and 16 cups flour, mix and knead gently. At 4 o'clock punch down. At 6 o'clock punch down. At 8 o'clock make into buns. Let rise overnight. Bake before 8 o'clock the next morning.

Mazzola Buns

from Judy Ridgway, Tahsis, B.C.

Makes 5 - 6 dozen
Temperature is 375°
Baking time is 20 minutes or till brown
Uses buttered muffin tins

Ingredients:
- 2 pkg. yeast
- 3/4 cup warm water
- 2 Tbsp. sugar
- 4 cups warm water
- 1/4 - 1/2 cup white sugar
- 2 eggs
- 1 cup vegetable or mazzola oil
- 2 Tbsp. salt
- 12 cups white flour

Method:
Dissolve yeast in 3/4 cup warm water with 2 Tbsp. sugar. Add yeast mixture to water, sugar, oil, eggs, salt in large bowl. Mix. Add 4 cups of flour at a time, until stiff dough. Let rise about one hour. Punch down and let rise again. Place in pans and let rise again then bake.

Two Hour Buns

from Edith Gibson, Victoria, B.C.

Temperature is 375°
Baking time is 15 - 20 minutes

Ingredients:
- 1 pkg. yeast
- 1 Tsp. sugar
- 1 cup warm water
- 1/2 cup sugar
- 1 Tbsp. salt
- 3 Tbsp. cooking oil
- 2 cups boiling water
- 3 eggs
- 7 cups flour

Method:
Mix 1 Tsp. sugar in with 1 cup warm water. Sprinkle yeast on top and let stand for 10 minutes. Combine sugar, salt, oil and pour over this boiling water. Let cool. Beat 3 eggs. Add and mix. Add flour. Mix well. Knead every 15 minutes for 2 hours. Make into buns. Let rise and bake.

Goofy Buns

from Fanny Carlile, Victoria, B.C.

Temperature is 350°
Baking time is 15 - 20 minutes

Ingredients:
1/2 cup shortening
1/3 cup sugar
1 egg
2 cups warm water
1 pkg. yeast
1 Tsp. salt
1 Tsp. baking powder
flour

Method:
Cream shortening, sugar and egg in a large bowl. Place yeast in warm water. Add to sugar mixture when yeast rises to top of water. Sift flour, salt and baking powder. Mix all together to form a soft dough. Knead well. Let stand until double in size (2 - 3 hours). Form into buns. Let rise again. Bake in greased pans until golden brown.

Overnight Buns

from Marlene Scott, Campbell River, BC

Temperature is 375°
Baking time is 15 minutes

Ingredients:
2 1/2 cups warm water
1/2 cup sugar
2 eggs, beaten
1/2 cup shortening or
    margarine
1 1/2 Tsp. salt
7 cups flour
1 pkg. yeast
1 Tsp. sugar
1/2 cup warm water

Method:
At 7 p.m. Combine 1 Tsp.sugar in 1/2 cup warm water. Sprinkle yeast in and let sit for 10 minutes. Then pour 2 cups water over marg, salt and sugar. Add 3 1/2 cups flour to make thin batter. Add eggs, yeast and remaining flour to make stiff dough. Punch bread dough down twice. 1 1/2 - 2 hours apart. Make buns on cookie sheet. Place in covered area away from drafts overnight. Bake in morning.

A similar recipe was submitted by Audrey Barnet–Port Coquitlam.

Whole Wheat Batter Bread

from Esperanza Kitchen

Temperature is 375°
Baking time is 40 minutes

Ingredients:
2 1/2 cups warm water
2 pkg. yeast
2 cups whole wheat flour
4 cups sifted white flour
4 Tsp. salt
1/4 cup shortening
1/4 cup brown sugar

Method:
Measure into large bowl warm water. Add yeast and stir to dissolve. Mix separately whole wheat flour and white flour, salt. To yeast water add half of flour mixture and shortening and brown sugar. Beat 2 minutes. Add remaining flour and mix well. Cover with wax paper and let rise until double. Punch down and divide into loaf pans. Let rise and bake.

Whole Wheat Bread

from Martha Holm, Powell River, B.C.

Makes 5 loaves
Temperature is 375°
Baking time is 30 - 35 minutes

Ingredients:
1 1/2 cups milk
1/2 cup brown sugar
2 Tbsp. salt
1/2 cup shortening
2 1/4 cups lukewarm
water
2 Tbsp. or 2 pkg. of yeast
1 cup lukewarm water
2 Tsp. sugar
6 cups whole wheat flour
6 - 6 1/2 cups white flour

Method:
Scald 1 1/2 cups milk then add 1/2 cup brown sugar, 2 Tbsp. salt, 1/2 cup shortening, then add 2 1/4 cups cold water (lukewarm). Dissolve in 1 cup warm water and 2 Tsp. sugar, 2 Tbsp. yeast. Add to first mixture. Add 6 cups whole wheat flour and beat till smooth. Add 6-6 1/2 cups white flour. Shape into a ball. Let rise till double. Punch down and shape into loaves. Let rise and cook at 375° for 30-35 minutes.

Notes

Home Baked Bread Sticks

from Isabel McPherson, Whitby, Ont.

Makes 2 dozen
Temperature is 350°F
Baking time is 20 minutes

Ingredients:

1 1/2 cups lukewarm
water
1 Tsp. sugar
2 Tbsp. yeast
1/4 cup vegetable oil
2 Tsp. salt
3 1/4 cups flour
1 egg white
1 Tbsp. water
Sesame seeds

Method:

In bowl combine 1/2 warm water and 1 Tsp. sugar. Sprinkle yeast over. Let stand till foamy. Add remaining sugar, oil, salt. Beat well. Alternately add flour and remaining water to make soft dough. Knead 5 min. till smooth. Cover for 5 min. Shape into 24 inch roll. Cut into 24 pieces. Cover and rest 5 min. With wet hands roll each piece to shape of pencil. Place 1 in. apart on pan. Brush on egg white & water. Sprinkle on seeds. Cover 10 min. Bake till brown/crisp.

Comment: Bake one sheet at a time KEEPING THE REMAINDER IN THE FRIDGE to prevent rising.

Sourdough Bread

from Marilyn McCall, Zeballos, B.C.

Makes 2 loaves
Temperature is 375°
Baking time is 30 minutes

Ingredients:

Sourdough Mixture:
  1 cup flour
  1 cup hot water
  1 Tbsp. yeast at room
    temperature
Bread mixture:
  1 Tbsp. yeast
  2 Tbsp. sugar
  2 Tsp. salt
  1 cup water
  4 - 5 cups flour

Method:

Next day: Place 1 Tbsp. yeast,sugar,salt in bowl with 1 cup hot water. Wait 10 min. Stir. Add sourdough mixture and 1 cup flour. Beat till smooth then add enough flour to make soft dough. Knead 8 - 10 min. Place in greased bowl, let rise till double. Punch down. Place in pans. Let rise 1 more hour. Bake.

Note:

Day before - combine sourdough mixture ingredients. Cover loosely.

Dumplings/Casserole Tops/Biscuits

Esperanza Kitchen

Ingredients:
1 cup flour
2 Tsp. cream of tartar
1 Tsp. soda
1 1/2 Tbsp. butter or
   margarine
milk
cheddar cheese (optional)

Method:
Combine ingredients using just enough milk to make dough right consistency. Bake.

Bisquick Mix

from Vera Stewart, Haiti

Ingredients:
5 cups flour
3 Tbsp. baking powder
1/2 cup dry powdered
   milk
1/2 Tsp. salt
1/2 cup + 2 Tbsp. Crisco
   shortening

Method:
Mix well and store in tupperware in your fridge.

Aunt Tina's Biscuits

from Ruth Glaze, Victoria, B.C.

Temperature is 425°F
Baking time is 15 - 20 minutes

Ingredients:
2 cups flour
4 Tsp. baking powder
2 Tbsp. sugar
1/2 Tsp. salt
1/2 cup margarine
milk

Method:
Mix all ingredients together - add milk until dough is sticky. Then knead and roll out, cut and bake.

Muffins & Scones

Orange Blender Muffins

from Elaine Stoik, Vancouver, B.C.

Temperature is 400°
Baking time is 20 minutes

Ingredients:
1 orange
1/2 cup orange juice
1 egg
1/2 cup margarine
1 1/2 cups flour
1 Tsp. baking powder
1 Tsp. soda
3/4 cup sugar
dash of salt
1/2 cup raisins

Method:
Blend whole orange in blender. Add margarine, eggs and fruit. Blend. Mix dry ingredients. Add blender mixture to dry ingredients. Mix till smooth. Put into muffins tins and bake.

Ward's Camp Bran Muffins

from Nancy Symington, Tofino, B.C.

Makes 2 dozen
Temperature is 375°
Baking time is 15 minutes

Ingredients:
1 cup margarine
2 cups brown sugar
2 Tbsp. molasses
1/4 Tsp. salt
1 1/2 cups bran
2 cups buttermilk
2 Tsp. soda
2 Tsp. baking powder
2 3/4 cups flour
1 cup walnuts
1/2 cup raisins
2 beaten eggs

Method:
Cream margarine, brown sugar, eggs together. Add molasses and salt. Mix well. Combine bran, soda and buttermilk. Add to mixture. Combine baking powder, flour. Add to above mixture. Carefully fold in walnuts and raisins. Bake.

Delicious Bran Muffins

from Ruth Glaze, Victoria, B.C.

Temperature is 400°
Baking time is 15 minutes

Ingredients:
1/4 cup shortening or
   margarine
1/2 cup brown sugar
1/4 cup (or less) molasses
2 eggs
1 cup milk
1 1/2 cups bran
1 cup flour
1 1/2 Tsp. soda
3/4 Tsp. salt
raisins

Method:
Cream margarine and brown sugar together. Add molasses, eggs, milk and bran. Then stir in flour, baking soda, salt and raisins. Bake.

Bran Muffins

from Elaine Stoik, Vancouver, B.C.

Temperature is 400°
Baking time is 15 minutes

Ingredients:
1 1/2 cups bran
1 cup buttermilk
1/3 cup oil
1 egg
1/2 cup brown sugar
1/2 Tsp. vanilla
1 Tsp. baking powder
1 Tsp. baking soda
1/2 Tsp. salt
1 cup flour
1/2 cup raisins

Method:
Combine bran, buttermilk and oil and let stand. Mix together egg, brown sugar and vanilla and add to bran mixture. Mix the baking powder, baking soda, salt, flour and raisins and add to above mixture. Bake.

Honey Whole Wheat Muffins

from Laura Brisbane, Bellingham, Wash.

Makes 1 dozen
Temperature is 350°
Baking time is 25 minutes

Ingredients:
- 3 cups whole wheat flour
- 3/4 cup honey
- 1 cup milk
- 1/2 cup oil
- 1 egg
- 1/4 cup molasses
- 1 Tsp. soda

Method:
Combine ingredients and bake.

Date Whole Wheat Muffins

from Doris Kreller, Errington, B.C.

Makes 1 dozen
Temperature is 350°
Baking time is 15 - 20 minutes

Ingredients:
- 1 cup chopped dates
- 3/4 cup boiling water
- 1 Tsp. soda
- 2 Tbsp. butter
- 1/2 cup walnuts
- 1 large or 2 small eggs
- 1/2 cup brown sugar
- 1 cup whole wheat flour
- 1/4 Tsp. salt

Method:
Dissolve soda in boiling water. Then pour boiling water over dates, butter and walnuts. Set aside to cool. In separate bowl combine egg and sugar. Add to cooled mixture and then add flour and salt. Bake.

Pumpkin Muffins

from Alma Cunningham, Victoria, B.C.

Temperature is 350°
Baking time is 20 minutes

Ingredients:

1 cup pumpkin pulp
1 cup sugar
1/2 cup oil
1 egg
1 1/2 cups flour
1 Tsp. cinnamon
1 Tsp. baking soda
1 Tsp. baking powder
1/4 Tsp. salt
1/2 cup raisins

Method:

Mix pumpkin, sugar, oil and egg together. Add flour, cinnamon soda, baking powder, salt and raisins. Mix till moistened.

Another option is to sprinkle with brown sugar before baking.

A similar recipe was also submitted by Kathy Harmsworth–Esperanza.

Banana Muffins

from Hazel Benner, Quebec

Makes 18 muffins
Temperature is 350°
Baking time is 15 - 20 minutes

Ingredients:

3 - 4 ripe bananas (1 cup)
6 Tbsp. vegetable oil
1/2 cup sugar
1 Tsp. salt
1 well beaten egg
1 Tsp. vanilla
1 1/2 cups flour
1 Tsp. baking soda
1 Tsp. baking powder
1/2 cup chopped nuts

Method:

Mash bananas. Add oil, sugar and salt. Mix well. Add egg and vanilla. Beat well. Mix flour, soda and baking powder and add to mixture. Add nuts. Bake.

(Suggestion - use ice cream scoop to fill muffin tins.)

This recipe was also submitted by Alma Cunningham of Victoria.

Anytime Muffins

from Karin Hardy, Victoria, B.C.

Makes 5 - 6 dozen
Temperature is 375°
Baking time is 15 - 20 minutes

Ingredients:
2 cups rolled oats
2 cups boiling water
4 eggs, beaten
2 cups sugar (I use 1 -
  1 1/2 cups
1 cup oil
1 quart buttermilk
3 cups whole wheat flour
2 cups all purpose flour
5 Tsp. baking soda
1 Tsp. salt
4 cups bran

Method:
Combine oats and boiling water. Let cool. Mix together eggs, oil, sugar and buttermilk. Stir in sifted dry ingredients and bran just till moistened. Store in covered container in fridge till needed.

Pineapple Carrot Muffins

from Dave Frewing, NewWestminster, B.C.

Temperature is 350°
Baking time is 25 minutes

Ingredients:
3 cups flour
1 cup sugar
2 Tsp. baking powder
2 Tsp. baking soda
1 Tsp. salt
2 Tsp. cinnamon
1 cup salad oil
4 medium eggs, well
  beaten
2 Tsp. vanilla
2 cups finely grated carrot
1 cup crushed pineapple
  with juice

Method:
Mix together flour, sugar, baking powder, soda, salt and cinnamon. Combine oil, eggs, vanilla. Add flour. Stir just until dry ingredients are moistened. Stir in grated carrots and pineapple. Bake.

Refrigerator Muffins

from Hazel Benner, Quebec

Temperature is 375°
Baking time is 10 - 15 minutes

Ingredients:
- 1 cup margarine
- 4 eggs
- 1 cup sugar
- 1 cup molasses
- 4 cups flour
- 1 cup milk or sour cream
- 1 Tsp. salt
- 1 Tsp. soda
- 1 Tsp. baking powder
- 1 Tsp. all spice
- 1 Tsp. cinnamon
- 4 Tsp. ginger
- 1 Tsp. vanilla

Method:
Cream margarine. Add sugar. Add eggs one at a time. Add molasses. Add soda to sour cream and vanilla. Mix flour, salt, baking powder and spices. Add flour mixture to milk mixture alternately to first mixture. Turn into muffin tins and let set overnight (24 hours).

Cheese Puffs

from Myrna Hill, M/V Anastasis - YWAM

Makes 12 puffs
Temperature is 450°
Baking time is 10 - 15 minutes
Uses buttered muffin tins

Ingredients:
- 2 egg
- 1/2 Tsp. salt
- 1 cup milk
- 1 cup grated cheese
- 1 small grated onion
- 1 rasher of chopped bacon
- 2 cups flour
- 4 Tsp. baking powder

Method:
Beat eggs with salt and milk. Add cheese, onion and bacon. Stir. Add flour and baking powder. Mix well together. Batter is medium - stiff but spoon into greased muffin tins.Bake.

Note: Tasty with soup and salad luncheons. Serve with butter.

Scones

from Alma Cunningham, Victoria, B.C.

Temperature is 350°
Baking time is 15 minutes

Ingredients:
- 3 cups flour
- 6 Tsp. baking powder
- 1 Tsp. salt
- 6 Tbsp. sugar
- 3/4 cup raisins
- 1/2 cup shortening
- 2 eggs

Method:
I use a knife or fork not my hands. To mix the shortening with the dry ingredients beat the eggs with a fork in a one cup measure. Fill cup with milk. Add to dry mixture. Add raisins. Pat and roll out and cut. Bake.

Top of the Stove Griddle Scones

from Jean Klym, Nanaimo, B.C.

Makes 12 - 15 scones

Ingredients:
- 2 cups flour
- 1/2 cup white sugar
- 1/2 Tsp. salt
- 3 Tsp. baking powder
- 1/2 cup butter or margarine
- 1 egg, slightly beaten
- 1/2 - 2/3 cup milk

Method:
Cut butter in dry ingredients with pastry blender until small meal consistency. Add beaten egg to milk. Add to dry mix making a well and stirring in. Drop from spoon (batter size of large egg) into frying pan or griddle. Cover with lid, cook till golden brown on each side.

Welsh Tea Cakes

from Vivian Burnie, Wales

Makes 28
Cooking time is 2 - 3 minutes each side
Uses an oiled griddle

Ingredients:
1 1/2 cups flour
1/2 cup margarine
1/3 cup sugar
1/2 cup currants or raisins
pinch of salt
2 Tsp. baking powder
1 egg
1 or 2 Tbsp. milk

Method:
Sift flour, salt and baking powder together. Rub in margarine. Add sugar and currants. Bind with egg and milk if it doesn't hold together well enough. On floured board roll out to 1/4 inch thickness. Cut into 2 1/2 inch rounds. Bake on griddle, low to middle heat. Welsh cakes can be served hot or cold, spread with butter, jam or for an extra treat top with whipped cream. This is a favourite of Welsh people.

French Breakfast Muffins

from Lois Hooks, Edmonton, Alberta

Makes 15
Temperature is 350°
Baking time is 20 - 25 minutes

Ingredients:
1/3 cup margarine
1/2 cup sugar
1 egg
1 1/2 cups flour
1 1/2 Tsp. baking powder
1/2 Tsp. salt
1/4 Tsp. nutmeg
1/2 cup milk
Topping: 1/2 cup sugar
1 Tsp. cinnamon
1/2 cup melted margarine

Method:
Mix shortening, sugar and egg well. Stir in dry ingredients alternately with milk. Bake. Topping - roll hot muffins in melted margarine then in the 1/2 cup sugar and cinnamon mixture. Serve warm.

Surprise Chocolate Muffins

from Nancy Symington, Tofino, B.C.

Makes 1 dozen
Temperature is 375°
Baking time is 20 minutes - don't overbake!

Ingredients:
- 1 - 3 oz. pkg. cream cheese
- 2 Tbsp. sugar
- 1 cup flour
- 1/2 cup sugar
- 3 Tbsp. unsweetened cocoa
- 2 Tsp. baking powder
- 1/2 Tsp. salt
- 1 egg, beaten
- 3/4 cup milk
- 1/3 cup cooking oil
- powdered sugar (optional)

Method:

In small bowl beat cream cheese and 2 teaspoons sugar until light and fluffy. Set aside. In large bowl stir together flour, sugar, cocoa, baking powder and salt. Make a well in centre of dry ingredients. Combine egg, milk and oil. Add all at once to dry ingredients, stirring just until moistened. Batter should be lumpy. Spoon about 2 tablespoons of chocolate batter into muffin pan. Drop 1 teaspoon cream cheese on top then more batter. Bake.

Notes

Mrs. O'Leary's Chocolate Cake

from Rhea Ready, Vancouver, B.C.

Temperature is 350°
Baking time is 45 minutes
Uses a 9 x 13 inch pan, buttered

Ingredients:
  2 cups flour
  1 Tsp. baking powder
  1/2 cup cocoa
  1 Tsp. salt
  2 cups sugar
  1/2 cup oil
  2 eggs (put in 2 cup
    measure)
  buttermilk or sour milk -
    enough to fill remainder
    of 2 cup measure
  2 Tsp. vanilla

Method:
Measure all ingredients into a bowl.
Beat until smooth. Drop 12 times.
(To make buttermilk or sour milk
add one tablespoon of lemon juice or
vinegar to sweet milk.) Bake.

Sharon's Crumb Cake

from Sharon Gerber, Alix, Alberta

Temperature is 325°
Baking time is 50 - 60 minutes
Uses a 9 inch pan, buttered

Ingredients:
  2 cups flour
  3/4 cup butter
  1 cup white sugar
  1 cup sour milk
  1 Tsp. soda
  1/2 Tsp. cloves
  1 Tsp. cinnamon
  1 egg
  1 cup raisins or currants

Method:
Rub together flour, butter and sugar
to crumb. Set aside 3/4 cup for topping. Mix remainder with sour milk,
soda, cloves, cinnamon, egg and
raisins. Spread with remaining 3/4
cup crumbs. Bake. (Note - a multiple
of 3 fills one 12 x 18 inch pan.)

Boiled Raisin Cupcakes

from Elsie Lindholm, Camrose, Alta.

Temperature is 350°
Baking time is 20 minutes

Ingredients:
1/2 cup shortening or
  margarine
1 1/2 cups brown sugar
2 eggs
3 cups flour
2 Tsp. cinnamon
1/2 Tsp. cloves
1/2 Tsp. salt
1 1/2 Tsp. baking soda
3 cups raisins
nuts (optional)

Method:
Simmer raisins with water for 20 minutes. Save one cup of raisin water. Cream margarine and brown sugar. Add eggs and beat well. Sift dry ingredients together and add alternately with raisin water. Last add raisins and nuts. Bake.

Torte

from Coastal Missions, Chemainus, B.C.

Serves 8 - 10
Temperature is 400°
Baking time is 10 - 12 minutes
Uses a Flan pan, buttered

Ingredients:
3 eggs
1 cup sugar
3 Tbsp. milk
1 1/3 cup flour
1/2 Tsp. salt
1 1/2 Tsp. baking powder

Method:
Beat eggs till thick. Add sugar slowly. Beat. Add liquid gradually. Beat. Sift flour, measure and add salt and baking powder. Sift. Slowly fold in flour mixture into egg mixture. (Wire whisk works well.) Pour into flan pan. Bake. Cool.

Mocha Cakes

from Hilda McPherson, Meaford, Ont.

Ingredients:
- 1 plain white cake mix
- unsalted peanuts
- Butter Icing

Method:
Mix cake mix according to package directions. Bake in small cup cake tins. Make a very thin butter icing (very runny). Grind peanuts very fine. Dip cupcakes in icing and roll in ground nuts. A Christmas tradition.

Chocolate Zucchini Cake

from Betty Harmsworth, Sidney, B.C.

Temperature is 325°
Baking time is 45 minutes or more
Uses a 9 x 12 inch pan

Ingredients:
- 1/2 cup margarine
- 1/2 cup oil
- 1 3/4 cups sugar
- 2 eggs
- 2 1/2 cups flour
- 4 Tbsp. cocoa
- 1/2 Tsp. baking powder
- 1 Tsp. soda
- 1/2 Tsp. cinnamon
- 1/2 Tsp. cloves
- 1/2 cup sour milk
- 2 cups finely grated zucchini, peel on
- 1/4 cup chocolate chips

Method:
Cream margarine and oil. Add sugar and eggs. Alternate dry ingredients with milk. Stir in zucchini. Sprinkle chips on top. Bake. Nice and moist!

Oatmeal Cake

from Donna Paracy, Tahsis, B.C.

Temperature is 350°
Baking time is 50 - 55 minutes
Uses a 9 x 13 inch greased pan

Ingredients:
- 1 1/4 cups boiling water
- 1 cup oatmeal
- 1/2 cup margarine (soft)
- 1 cup white sugar
- 1 cup brown sugar
- 1 Tsp. vanilla
- 2 eggs
- 1 1/2 cups flour
- 1 Tsp. soda
- 1/2 Tsp. salt
- 3/4 Tsp. cinnamon
- 1/4 Tsp. nutmeg

Method:
Pour boiling water over oatmeal and sit 20 minutes. Cream butter and beat in sugar till fluffy. Add vanilla and eggs. Add oats. Sift dry ingredients and add to cream mixture. Bake. Icing recipe follows.

Topping

from Donna Paracy, Tahsis, B.C.

Broil

Ingredients:
- 1/2 cup melted margarine
- 3 Tbsp. evaporated milk
- 1/2 cup brown sugar
- 1/3 cup nuts
- 3/4 cup coconut

Method:
Mix topping ingredients. Spread over top of cake when done. Put under broiler till bubbly.

Yule Cake

from Bethine Flynn, Seattle, Wash.

Temperature is 300°
Baking time is 1 1/2 - 2 hours
Uses a 2 paper-lined 9 inch loaf pans

Ingredients:
- 1 1/2 cups (8 oz) Brazil nuts
- 1 1/2 cups (8 oz) whole walnuts
- 1/2 lb. pitted dates
- 16 oz. pk. green/red maraschino cherries
- 1/2 cup seedles raisins
- 2 cups sifted flour
- 1 1/2 cups white sugar
- 1 Tsp. baking powder
- 1 Tsp. salt
- 6 eggs
- 2 Tsp. vanilla or almond flavouring

Method:
Mix fruits and nuts. Add flour, sugar and dry ingredients. Add beaten eggs and flavouring. Bake.

Saucepan Raisin Spice Cake

from Laura Brisbane, Bellingham, Wash.

Temperature is 350°
Baking time is 25 - 30 minutes
Uses a 8 inch square pan, buttered

Ingredients:
- 1 cup sugar
- 1/2 cup margarine
- 1 Tsp. cinnamon
- 1 Tsp. powdered cloves
- 1 Tsp. baking soda
- 1/2 Tsp. salt
- 1 cup dark raisins
- 1 cup water
- 1/2 cup chopped nuts (optional)

Method:
In medium saucepan cook over medium heat until margarine melts. Add sugar, cinnamon, cloves, salt, raisins, water, nuts. Let cool. Add flour, baking soda. Blend well. Bake. Ice and cut into squares.

Mom Sadler's Junk Cake

from Ruth Sadler, Tofino, B.C.

Serves 12
Temperature is 325°
Baking time is 70 minutes
Uses a 10 inch tube pan, buttered

Ingredients:
1/2 cup margarine
1 cup white sugar
2 eggs
1 1/2 Tsp. almond flavouring
2 cups flour
3 Tsp. baking powder
1/4 Tsp. salt
1/4 Tsp. mace
1/3 Tsp. cinnamon
1/4 Tsp. nutmeg
1/4 cup cloves
1/2 cup raisins
1/3 cup peel
1/3 cup dates
3/4 cup currants
2/3 cup milk

Method:
Beat together margarine, sugar and eggs. Mix together dry ingredients and beat alternately with the milk into the first mixture. Add almond flavouring. Add fruit and place in tube pan. Bake.

Dutch Butter Cake

from Ruth Glaze, Victoria, B.C.

Temperature is 325°
Baking time is 20 - 30 minutes
Uses a Pie plate

Ingredients:
1 cup white sugar
1 1/2 Tsp. almond flavouring
1 egg, beaten
1 1/2 cups flour
1/2 Tsp. baking powder
2/3 cup margarine or butter

Method:
Mix margarine, sugar and almond flavouring together. Add egg except for two tablespoons full. Then add flour and baking powder. Press into pie plate or pan and brush remaining egg on top. Sprinkle with a little sugar. Bake.

Banana Cake

from Rhea Ready, Vancouver, B.C.

Temperature is 325°
Baking time is 60 - 75 minutes
Uses a 12 cup tube pan, buttered

Ingredients:
- 1 cup oil
- 1/2 cup white sugar
- 1 cup packed brown sugar
- 3 eggs
- 1/3 cup orange juice
- 1 Tsp. vanilla
- 2 cups flour
- 2 Tsp. baking powder
- 1 Tsp. baking soda
- 1/2 Tsp. salt
- 1 cup bananas (about 3 medium)
- 1/2 cup raisins

Method:
Mix together until slightly thickened - oil, white and brown sugar, eggs, orange juice and vanilla. Add and beat for two minutes - flour, baking powder, baking soda and salt. Beat in bananas. Stir in raisins. Bake. Cool in pan 15 minutes before turning out to cool completely.

Refrigerator Fruit Cake

from Lou Harris, Union Bay, B.C.

Uses 2 loaf pans lined with wax paper

Ingredients:
- 1 lb. graham cracker crumbs
- 1 lb. marshmallows
- 1/4 lb. butter or margarine
- 1/2 cup fruit juice
- 1 lb. mixed candied fruits
- 1 lb. each of nuts & dates

Method:
Melt marshmallows, juice and butter in pan. Mix rest of ingredients in large bowl. Add marshmallow liquid. Mix completely. Pack in two loaf pans lined with wax paper. Let stand overnight.

Carrot Cake

from Sharon Gerber, Alix, Alberta

Temperature is 300°
Baking time is 60 minutes
Uses a 13 x 9 inch pan

Ingredients:
- 2 cups sugar
- 1 1/2 cups oil
- 4 eggs
- 2 1/2 cups flour
- 2 Tsp. salt
- 2 Tsp. baking soda
- 2 Tsp. cinnamon
- 4 cups grated carrots
- 1 1/2 cups chopped walnuts

Method:
Beat sugar, oil and eggs for two minutes. Sift dry ingredients together and add to oil mixture and beat at low speed one minute. Add carrots and nuts. Spread in pan. Bake. When cool ice with following recipe.

A similar recipe was also sent in by Beulah Harnam - Vancouver.

Cream Cheese Icing

from Sharon Gerber, Alix, Alberta

Ingredients:
- 1 cup icing sugar
- 1 - 8 oz. pkg. cream cheese*
- 1/4 cup butter
- 1 Tsp. vanilla

Method:
Beat all ingredients together thoroughly.

* Cream cheese should be at room temperature.

Carrot Cake

from Rhea Ready, Vancouver, B.C.

Temperature is 325°
Baking time is 60-75 minutes
Uses a 12 cup tube pan

Ingredients:
- 1 1/4 cups oil
- 1 cup white sugar
- 1 cup brown sugar
- 3 eggs
- 1/3 cup orange juice
- 1 Tsp. vanilla
- 2 cups flour
- 2 Tsp. baking powder
- 1 Tsp. baking soda
- 2 Tsp. cinnamon
- 1/2 Tsp. nutmeg
- 1/4 Tsp.ginger
- 1/4 Tsp. cloves
- 1/2 Tsp. salt
- 3 cups grated carrots
- 1/2 cup chopped nuts

Method:
Beat together oil, sugar, eggs orange juice and vanilla. Then add dry ingredients together and beat for two minutes. Finally, add carrots and nuts. Spread in pan. Bake. Cool 15 minutes before turning out to cool.

Crumb Cake

from Bernice Bolton, Gold River, B.C.

Temperature is 350°
Baking time is 30 minutes
Uses an 8 x 8 inch pan, buttered

Ingredients:
- 2 cups flour
- 1 cup raisins
- 1 egg
- 1 cup sour milk
- 1 Tsp. cinnamon
- 3/4 cup butter
- 1 Tsp. cloves
- 1 cup white sugar
- 1 Tsp. soda

Method:
Rub flour, sugar and butter into crumbs. Remove one cup for top. Mix remainder of ingredients and pour into prepared pan. Sprinkle with reserrved crumbs. Bake.

Old Family Applesauce Cake Recipe

from Karin Hardy, Victoria, B.C.

Temperature is 375°
Baking time is 45 - 50 minutes
Uses a 9 x 13 inch pan, buttered and floured

Ingredients:
1/2 cups shortening
1 1/2 cups sugar
1 1/2 cups thick apple-
sauce
1 cup chopped nuts
2 cups raisins
2 1/2 cups flour
2 Tsp. baking soda
1/2 Tsp. salt
1/2 Tsp. cinnamon
1/2 Tsp. nutmeg

Method:
Cream shortening and sugar. Add applesauce and mix well. Sift dry ingredients. Add with nuts and raisins. Dough will be thick. Bake. Ice with butter icing.

Midnight Chocolate Cake

from Gail Celester, Tofino, B.C.

Temperature is 350°
Baking time is 55 minutes
Uses a 9 or 13 inch pan, buttered

Ingredients:
1/2 cup shortening
1 1/4 cups sugar
2 eggs, well beaten
1 Tsp. vanilla
1 1/2 cups flour
1 Tsp. soda
1 Tsp. baking powder
pinch salt
1 cup hot water
1/2 cup cocoa

Method:
Beat shortening and sugar till fluffy. Add well beaten eggs and vanilla. Sift together flour, soda, baking powder and salt and add to creamed mixture alternately with cocoa and water.

Syrian Nutmeg Cake

from Betsy Patton, Bellingham, Wash.

Temperature is 350°
Baking time is 40 minutes
Uses a 9 inch square pan, generously buttered

Ingredients:
- 2 cups brown sugar
- 2 cups flour
- 1/2 cup butter
- 1 Tsp. nutmeg
- 1/2 Tsp. salt
- 1 cup sour cream
- 1 egg
- 1 Tsp. soda
- 1/2 cup chopped nuts

Method:
Combine brown sugar, flour, butter, salt and nutmeg in mixing bowl. Blend until crumbly and completely mixed. Spoon half of mixture into well greased pan. Stir soda into sour cream. Mix into remaining crumbs with egg. Pour batter over crumbs and sprinkle with chopped nuts. Serve warm with whipped cream or cool with fruit or ice cream.

Oatmeal Chocolate Cake

from Joan Clunies-Ross, Langley, B.C.

Temperature is 350°
Baking time is 35 minutes
Uses an 8 or 9 inch square pan, buttered

Ingredients:
- 1/2 cup rolled oats
- 1/2 cup butter or margarine
- 4 Tbsp. cocoa
- 1 cup boiling water
- 1 1/4 cups brown sugar
- 2 eggs
- 1 cup flour
- 3/4 Tsp. baking soda
- 1 1/2 Tsp. baking powder
- 1/2 Tsp. vanilla
- pinch of salt

Method:
Place oats, butter and cocoa in a bowl. Pour in boiling water. Stir gently then let sit for 15 minutes. Add the remaining ingredients. Bake. This is a moist dark cake.

Lazy Lady Cake

from Joan Clunies-Ross, Langley, B.C.

Temperature is 350°
Baking time is 25 minutes
Uses an 8 or 9 inch square pan not buttered

Ingredients:
2 eggs
3/4 cup sugar
1 cup flour
1 Tsp. baking powder
1/4 Tsp. salt
1 Tsp. vanilla
1/2 cup milk
1 Tbsp. butter

Method:
Beat eggs until fluffy. Add sugar.
Add dry ingredients. Bring milk and
butter to boiling point. Add to other
mixture. Put in pan. Ice with following recipe.

Icing for Lazy Lady Cake

from Joan Clunies-Ross, Langley, B.C.

Ingredients:
5 Tbsp. brown sugar
2 Tbsp. butter
2 Tbsp. cream
1/2 cup fine coconut

Method:
Bring to melting point. Spread on
cake when it is cooked and brown it
a little in the oven.

One Bowl Brownie Pie

from Nancy Symington, Tofino, B.C.

Temperature is 350°
Baking time is 30 minutes
Uses a pie pan, buttered

Ingredients:
2 eggs
1 cup sugar
1/2 cup soft margarine
1/2 cup flour
3 Tbsp. cocoa
1 Tsp. vanilla
1/4 Tsp. salt
1/2 cup chopped walnuts

Method:
Dump everything except nuts into one bowl. Beat for four minutes. Add nuts and pour into pie pan. Bake. (Pie will settle down in the middle as it cools. That's alright - it doesn't hurt the taste.)

Poppy Seed Bread

from Diane Bradford, Tofino, B.C.

Temperature is 350°
Baking time is 50 - 60 minutes
Uses 9x5 inch loaf pans, buttered

Ingredients:

2 1/4 cups all purpose
   flour
3/4 cup sugar
3/4 cup poppy seed
1 Tbsp. baking powder
3 eggs
1 1/4 cups milk
3/4 cup vegetable oil
1 Tsp. vanilla

Method:

Combine flour, sugar, poppy seeds and baking powder in a bowl. Beat eggs, milk, oil and vanilla. Add dry ingredients and stir until smooth. Pour batter into prepared pans. Bake until tester comes out smooth.

Banana Quick Bread

from Alma Cunningham, Victoria, B.C.

Temperature is 350°
Baking time is 50 minutes or till done
Uses greased loaf pans

Ingredients:

1 3/4 cups flour
2 3/4 Tsp. baking powder
1/4 Tsp. salt
1/2 cup chopped nuts
1/3 cup shortening
2/3 cup sugar
2 beaten eggs
1 cup mashed bananas
1 cup mixed fruit & peel
1/4 cup raisins

Method:

Sift together into a large bowl flour, baking powder and salt. Combine and add mashed bananas and sugar. Combine and beat eggs, and shortening. Add nuts. Pour the liquid mixture into the bowl. Combine all ingredients with a few swift strokes. Stir lightly until barely blended. Bake.

Lettuce Loaf

from Nadine Kruger, Campbell River, B.C.

Temperature is 375°F
Baking time is 55 minutes
Uses a loaf pan, buttered

Ingredients:

1 cup finely chopped
    lettuce
1 1/2 cups sifted flour
2 Tsp. Baking powder
1/2 Tsp. salt
1/4 Tsp. mace
1/4 Tsp. ginger
1 cup sugar
1/2 cup oil
1/2 Tsp. baking soda
1 1/2 Tsp. grated lemon
    rind
2 eggs
1/2 cup chopped walnuts

Method:

Put lettuce in blender with 2 - 3
Tbsp. water and put on highest
setting. Walnuts can be added to
save you chopping by hand. Sift
flour, baking powder, soda, salt and
spices together. Combine sugar, oil
and lemon rind in one bowl then
mix in flour mixture then lettuce.
Add eggs one at a time beating well.
Stir in walnuts if separate from
lettuce. Pour into loaf pan. Bake.

Orange Bread

from Hilda McPherson, Meaford, Ontario

Temperature is 350°F
Baking time is 50 minutes
Uses a buttered loaf pan

Ingredients:

Peelings of two oranges
cold water
1 cup sugar
1/2 cup sugar
1 Tbsp. butter
1 unbeaten egg
1 cup milk
3 cups flour
4 Tsps. baking powder

Method:

Cut peeling of oranges in tiny
pieces. Cover with cold water. Set
on stove and simmer (not boil) three
times. Drain off water and add fresh
water each time. Add 1 cup sugar.
Stir to melt sugar. Cream together
half cup sugar, butter. Add egg,
peelings, milk and flour which has
been sifted with baking powder. Let
mixture stand 20 minutes. Bake.

Zucchini Bread

from Barbara Haskell, Three Hills, Alberta

Temperature is 325°F
Baking time is 60 minutes
Uses 2 buttered loaf pans

Ingredients:
- 2 cups sugar
- 3 eggs
- 1 cup cooking oil
- 1 Tsp. vanilla
- 2 cups zucchini
- 3 cups flour
- 1 Tsp. baking soda
- 1 Tsp. baking powder
- 1/2 Tsp. salt
- 1 Tsp. cinnamon
- 1 Tsp. cloves
- 1 Tsp. nutmeg
- 1/2 cup raisins

Method:

Blend first four ingredients in mixer. Fold in finely grated zucchini. Add dry ingredients. Fold in raisins. Place in two prepared loaf pans. Bake.

Zucchini Loaf

from Cathy Birtles, Calgary, Alberta

Temperature is 350°
Baking time is approximately 60 minutes
Uses 2 loaf pans, buttered

Ingredients:
- 2 cups grated zucchini (unpeeled)
- 3 cups flour
- 3 Tsp. cinnamon
- 1 Tsp. baking soda
- 1 Tsp.salt
- 3/4 Tsp. baking powder
- 1 cup oil
- 1 3/4 - 2 cups white sugar
- 4 eggs

Method:

Combine flour, cinnamon, baking soda, salt and baking powder. Cream sugar, oil and eggs. Add to flour mixture. Then add zucchini. Bake till toothpick inserted in comes out clean.

Quick Orange Bread

from Louise Karllson, Calgary, Alberta

Makes 2 loaves
Temperature is 350°
Baking time is 50 minutes or till done
Uses greased loaf pans

Ingredients:

- 3 cups sifted all-purpose flour
- 3 Tsp. baking powder
- 1/2 Tsp. salt
- 1 Tbsp. grated orange rind
- 1/2 - 3/4 cup sugar
- 1 egg
- 1/4 cup orange juice
- 1 1/4 cups milk
- 2 Tbsp. melted shortening
- 1 cup chopped/broken nutmeats

Method:

Sift together into a large bowl flour, baking powder and salt. Combine and add orange rind and sugar (For a more cake-like result, use the larger amount of sugar). Combine and beat egg, orange juice, milk, and shortening. Add nuts. Pour the liquid mixture into the bowl. Combine all ingredients with a few swift strokes. Stir lightly until barely blended. Bake in 2 loaf pans.

Lemon or Orange Loaf

from Audrey Lore, NewWestminster, B.C.

Temperature is 350°F
Baking time is 60 minutes
Uses a buttered loaf pan

Ingredients:

- 6 Tbsp. margarine
- 1 cup white sugar
- 1/2 cup milk
- 1 1/2 cups flour
- 1 1/2 Tsp baking powder
- grated rind from 2 lemons/oranges
- juice of 2 lemons
- 1/2 cup sugar
- 1 beaten egg

Method:

Mix margarine, 1 cup white sugar, milk, flour, baking powder, lemon rind and beaten egg. Pour into loaf pan. Bake. When loaf is still hot, pour over top and sides the juice of two lemons mixed with the half cup of sugar. Bake.

Cookies and Squares

White Coconut Macaroons

from Doris Kreller, Errington, B.C.

Makes 36
Temperature is 300°
Baking time is 20-25 minutes

Ingredients:

3 egg whites at room
temperature
1 cup white sugar
2 Tbsp. corn starch
1/4 Tsp. salt
2 1/4 cups coconut (un-
sweetened)
1 Tsp. vanilla

Method:

Butter cookie sheet or cover cookie
sheet with rice paper. In top of
double boiler beat egg whites thoroughly. Sift sugar and corn starch
together and add small amount at a
time while finishing egg beating till
they are quite stiff. Put over hot (not
boiling) water and cook, stirring
constantly till mixture coats a silver
spoon. (About 15 minutes.) Remove
from hot water and add coconut,
salt and vanilla. Fold in. Drop on
pans with a teaspoon. (Don't make
them large.) Bake in slow oven till
thoroughly cooked.

Liz's Cluster Cookies

from Nancy Symington, Tofino, B.C.

Temperature is 350°
Baking time is 10-12 minutes
Uses an ungreased cookie sheet

Ingredients:

1 Tsp. vanilla
1 cup packed brown sugar
2/3 cup oil
1 egg
1 cup flour
1 Tsp. baking powder
1/2 Tsp. baking soda
1 1/4 cups oats
1/2 cup coconut

Method:

Mix together vanilla, brown sugar,
oil and egg. Combine flour, baking
powder and soda then add to mixture. Finally add oats and coconut
and stir well. Drop by teasponfuls
on cookie sheet.

Melting Moments

from Alma Cunningham, Victoria, B.C.

Temperature - moderate
Baking time – watch

Ingredients:
- 1 cup brown sugar
- 1 cup shortening
- 1 Tsp. soda
- 1/4 cup boiling water
- 2 cups oatmeal
- 2 cups flour
- vanilla

Method:
Dissolve soda in boiling water. Combine all ingredients. Roll in small balls in palm of hands and flatten with fork. Bake.

Molasses Cookies

from Alma Cunningham, Victoria, B.C.

Temperature is Moderate
Uses a cookie sheet

Ingredients:
- 1 cup shortening
- 1 cup white sugar
- 1 cup molasses
- 1 egg
- 1 Tsp. cream of tartar
- 4 Tsp. soda
- 3/4 cup water or tea
- 1 Tsp. salt
- 1 Tbsp. vanilla
- flour - enough to mix

Method:
Mix all ingredients together. Let stand overnight. Add more flour in morning if needed. Roll out and cut. Bake.

Breakfast Cookies

from Jean Hood, Matsqui, B.C.

Temperature is 350°
Baking time is 12 - 15 minutes
Uses a buttered cookie sheet

Ingredients:

1 cup lard/shortening/or
   margarine
1 cup brown sugar
1 egg
1/2 Tsp. soda
pinch of salt
2 1/2 cups oatmeal
1 1/2 cups flour
1 Tsp. vanilla
1/2 cup walnuts
1/2 cup raisins
1/2 cup chocolate chips

Method:

Cream shortening, sugar and egg together. Add combined dry ingredients and mix well. Stir in nuts, raisins and chocolate chips. Bake.

Uncooked Chocolate Clusters

from Esperanza Kitchen

Ingredients:

2 cups sugar
1/2 cup margarine
1/2 cup milk
1/2 cup cocoa
1 Tsp. vanilla
salt
3 cups oatmeal
1 cup coconut

Method:

Boil hard for five minutes sugar, margarine, milk, cocoa. Remove from heat and add vanilla, salt, oatmeal and coconut. Immediately drop by spoonfuls onto wax paper.

Christmas Coffee Dipped Dainties

from Isabel McPherson, Whitby, Ont.

Makes 8 1/2 dozen
Temperature is 375°
Baking time is 5-7 minutes
Uses an ungreased cookie sheet

Ingredients:
1 Tbsp. instant coffee
2 Tsp. boiling water
2 1/2 cups flour
1/2 Tsp. baking powder
1/4 Tsp. salt
1 cup margarine
1 cup sugar
1 egg
2 Tsp. lemon juice
1 Tsp. vanilla extract
Glaze (recipe follows)

Method:
In small measuring cup, combine instant coffee and water. Mix well and set aside. In a small bowl combine flour, baking powder and salt, set aside. In a large bowl beat margarine and sugar until creamy. Beat in egg, lemon juice, vanilla and coffee mixture. Gradually add flour mixture. Mix well. Roll into balls using 1 teaspoon dough for each. Place on cookie sheet. Flatten to about 1 1/2 inch diameter using glass bottom dipped in sugar. Cool completely.

Cookie Glaze

from Isabel McPherson, Whitby, Ont.

Ingredients:
4 Tbsp. instant coffee
6 Tbsp. boiling water
4 cups sifted icing sugar
2 Tsp. vanilla
1 1/2 cups ground pecans
   or walnuts

Method:
In a small bowl combine instant coffee and boiling water. Gradually add icing sugar and vanilla. Beat until creamy. Dip half cookie in glaze then in ground nuts.

Shortbread

from Lou Morrison, Victoria, B.C.

Temperature is 350°
Baking time is 15-18 minutes

Ingredients:
1 lb. butter (or 1/2 marg/ 1/2 butter)
1 cup light brown sugar
4 cups all purpose flour
1 Tsp. vanilla

Method:
Cream butter, sugar and vanilla. Add flour gradually. (The secret of good shortbread, if any, is in the kneading - you must knead and knead it.) Chill. Roll out and cut into favourite shapes. The cookies should be very light brown.

Whipped Shortbread

from Judy Ellis, Tahsis, B.C.

Makes 3 dozen
Temperature is 325°
Baking time is 15 minutes

Ingredients:
2 cups margarine (use 1/2 butter)
1 cup icing sugar
3 cups flour
1/2 cup cornstarch

Method:
Whip margarine till fluffy. Add remaining ingredients. Whip 15 minutes then drop by teaspoon onto white sugar (if desired). Place on ungreased cookie sheet. Garnish with a small bit of coloured cherry.

A similar recipe was also submitted by Judy Ridgway, Tahsis, B.C.

Shortbread

from Mames McPherson, Toronto, Ont.

Makes about 100
Temperature is 350°
Baking time is 20 minutes

Ingredients:
1 lb. butter
4 cups flour
1 cup rice flour
1 cup fruit sugar

Method:
Cream butter and sugar. Add flour gradually. Pat down on cookie sheet, touching all edges. Roll smooth with rolling pin. Bake 10 minutes. Remove and punch all over with a fork. Bake about 10 more minutes. Cut into rectangles.

Basic Cookie Mix

from Jewell Leighton, Duncan, B.C.

Temperature is 375°
Baking time is 10-15 minutes

BASIC

Ingredients:
8 cups all purpose flour
2 1/2 cups granulated sugar
2 cups brown sugar (packed)
4 Tsp. salt
1 1/2 Tsp. baking soda
3 cups vegetable shortening

Method:
In a large bowl combine dry ingredients, cut in shortening until evenly distributed. Store in a cool place. makes 16 cups of mix.

TO USE

1 Tbsp. of milk
1 Tsp. of vanilla (or other choice
1 egg
plus whatever else you wish - chocolate chips, nuts, raisins, etc.

makes 2 dozen

Method:
To use combine 3 cups of mix with milk vanilla eggs and any other favourite ingredient. Bake to make 2 dozen cookies.

Peanut Butter Chocolate Chip

from Audrey Barnett, Port Coquitlam, BC

Makes 4 dozen
Temperature is 350°
Baking time is 12 minutes

Ingredients:

1 cup margarine
1 cup peanut butter
1 cup brown sugar
2 cups flour
2 eggs
1 Tsp. baking power
1/2 Tsp. soda
1/2 Tsp. salt
6 oz. chocolate chips

Method:

Cream margarine and peanut butter. Add brown sugar. Add eggs. Beat well. Next add dry ingredients. Stir. Add chocolate chips. Drop by teaspoon on cookie sheet.

Sugar Cutouts

from Ann Hill, Nanaimo, B.C.

Makes 6 dozen
Temperature is 400°
Baking time is 5-8 minutes
Uses a greased cookie sheet

Ingredients:

3 1/2 cups flour
1 Tsp. baking powder
1/2 Tsp. salt
1 cup shortening
1 1/2 cups sugar
2 eggs, well beaten
1 1/2 Tsp. vanilla

Method:

Sift flour and baking powder. Add a dash of salt. Cream shortening and sugar until light. Beat in eggs and vanilla. Work flour into creamed mixture. Wrap in foil and chill. Roll out a bit at a time 1/8 inch thickness. Cut into shapes. Bake until firm - golden around edges. Decorate for appropriate holiday.

Surprise Cookies

from Barbara Lenderink, Surrey, B.C.

Temperature is 375°
Baking time is 10-12 minutes
Uses a buttered cookie sheet

Ingredients:
- 3 cups flour
- 1 Tsp. soda
- 1/2 Tsp. salt
- 1 cup butter
- 1/2 cup brown sugar
- 2 eggs, unbeaten
- 2 Tbsp. water
- 1 Tsp. vanilla
- 1 pkg solid chocolate mint wafers
- walnut halves

Method:
Sift flour, soda and salt. Cream butter, Add sugar. Blend in eggs, water and vanilla. Beat well. Add dry ingredients. Refrigerate for two hours. Enclose a chocolate mint wafer in about one tablespoon of chilled dough. Place on greased cookie sheet 2 inches apart. Top with walnut half.

Snow Balls

from Doris Kreller, Errington, B.C.

Makes 2 - 3 dozen balls

Ingredients:
- 1 cup peanut butter
- 1/2 cup icing sugar
- 1/2 cup non-instant milk powder
- 1/2 cup chopped mixed fruit (raisins, dates, cherries, etc.)
- 1/2 cup chopped nuts

Method:
Make into small balls and roll in thin icing then roll in coconut. Refrigerate.(You could use icing sugar instead of milk powder.) Make thin icing by combining 1/2 cup icing sugar and either milk or water to make a thin consistency.

Unbaked Peanut Butter Cereal Roll

from Doris Kreller, Errington, B.C.

Ingredients:
- 1 cup peanut butter
- 1 cup brown sugar
- 1 cup corn syrup
- 2 heaping cups corn flakes
- 2 heaping cups of crispy rice cereal

Method:
Put peanut butter, brown sugar and corn syrup in top of double boiler and melt over hot water. Add corn flakes and rice cereal. Mix well. Form into rolls. Wrap in waxed paper or plastic wrap. Refrigerate and slice as needed.

Oatmeal Cookies

from Colleen Shonwise, Tahsis, B.C.

Temperature is 375°
Baking time is 12-15 minutes
Uses a buttered cookie sheet

Ingredients:
- 1 cup melted butter
- 1 cup white sugar
- 1/2 cup brown sugar
- 1 Tsp. soda
- 1 Tsp. baking powder
- 1 beaten egg
- 1 1/4 cups oatmeal
- 3/4 cup coconut
- 1 1/2 cups flour

Method:
Mix all together in large pot in which butter was melted. Drop or place by spoonfuls onto greased cookie sheets. You can add chocolate chips, raisins, nuts or dates. If you add chocolate chips make sure butter is cool or they will melt.

A similar recipe was also submitted by Audrey Dol of Tahsis.

Cherry Surprises

from Audrey Barnett, Port Coquitlam, BC

Makes 5 doz. approx.

Ingredients:
- 1 cup butter or margarine
- 3 cups icing sugar
- 2 Tbsp. milk
- 2 Tsp. vanilla
- 3 cups fine or medium coconut
- cherries
- graham cracker crumbs

Method:
Mix first 5 ingredients well. Form into a ball with a cherry in centre. Roll in cracker crumbs. Refrigerate. (Freezes well.)

These are nice for Christmas.

Chocolate Dipped Raspberry Crisps

from Helen Ottom, Campbell River, B.C.

Makes 25 cookies
Temperature is 350°
Baking time is 10 - 12 minutes

Ingredients:
- 1 cup flour
- 1 cup finely chopped almonds
- 1/2 cup softened butter
- 6 Tbsp. granulated sugar
- 1 1/2 Tsp. vanilla
- 1/4 cup raspberry jam
- 2 squares semi-sweet chocolate

Method:
Blanch almonds. Combine flour, almonds stir well. Cream butter, sugar and vanilla together thoroughly. Stir in flour, almonds. Mix well. Use your hands to work mixture into a smooth dough. Shape and chill overnight or till firm.Cut roll in 1/4 inch slices and place on ungreased baking sheet. Bake. Cool. Spread half of cookies with 1/2 Tsp. jam (raspberry, strawberry, apricot). Top with remaining cookie.

Comment: You can line baking sheet with waxed paper and dip half of each filled cookie into melted chocolate. Place on wax paper. Let stand till set. Store in fridge.

Jan Hagel Cookies

from Jackie Vegt, Vancouver, B.C.

Temperature is 350°
Baking time is 20-30 minutes
Uses a buttered cookie sheet

Ingredients:
- 1 cup butter or margarine
- 1 cup sugar
- 1 cup white flour
- 1 cup whole wheat flour
- 1 egg
- 1/2 Tsp. baking soda
- 1 Tsp. cinnamon
- flaked almonds

Method:
Cream butter with sugar. Add all dry ingredients except nut flakes. Add egg except for a little egg white. Knead with hands. Spread and pat onto greased cookie sheet. Mix egg white with a little water and spread over top. Sprinkle with nut flakes.

Oatmeal Chocolate Chip Cookies

from Alma Cunningham, Victoria, B.C.

Temperature is 350°
Baking time is 10 - 12 minutes

Ingredients:
- 1 cup shortening
- 3/4 cup brown sugar
- 1/4 cup white sugar
- 1 Tsp. vanilla
- 1 1/2 cups flour
- 1/2 Tsp. salt
- 1 Tsp. soda
- 1/4 cup boiling water
- 2 cups oatmeal
- 1/2 cup chopped nuts
- 1 pkg. (16 oz.) chocolate chips

Method:
Mix dry ingredients. Add shortening and water, drop on cookie sheet and then flatten with a fork. Bake.

Plain Brownies

from Val Leong, Tahsis, B.C.

Temperature is 350°
Baking time is 15 minutes
Uses a buttered cookie sheet

Ingredients:
- 1 cup margarine
- 2 cups white sugar
- 1/4 cup cocoa
- 4 eggs
- 1 1/2 cups flour
- 1 Tsp. salt
- 2 Tsp. vanilla

Method:
In pot melt margarine. Remove from heat and add and beat sugar, cocoa, and eggs. Add flour, salt and vanilla. Pour onto pan. Bake.Cool. Slice into bars.

Lazy Raisin Bars

from Jenny Jackson, Creston, B.C.

Temperature is 375°
Cooking time is 20 - 25 minutes
Uses a buttered cookie sheet

Ingredients:
- 2 eggs
- 2 cups brown sugar
- 1 cup shortening
- 1 cup raisins
- 3 cups flour
- 1 Tsp. cinnamon
- 1 Tsp. soda
- 1 Tsp. baking powder
- 1 cup boiling water

TOPPING:
- 4 Tbsp. sugar
- 2 Tsp. cinammon

Method:
Measure first 9 ingredients into large bowl in order listed. Do not stir until all are in the bowl. Beat thoroughly. Spread 1/4 inch thick onto cookie sheet. Sprinkle with the sugar and cinammon mixed together for the topping. Bake.

A similar recipe also submitted by Pearl Cochrane–Comox, B.C.

Danish Almond Slice

from Hanne Reid, Steinbeck, Man.

Makes 48 squares
Temperature is 375°
Baking time is 20 - 30 minutes
Uses a buttered 9 x 13 inch or 8 x 8 inch pan

Ingredients:

6 egg yolks
1 1/3 cups sugar
1 3/4 cups margarine, softened
2 Tsp. baking powder
4 cups flour
6 egg whites
3 cups icing sugar
2 cups bread crumbs
2 Tbsp. almond flavouring

Method:

Beat egg yolks and sugar well. Add margarine. Mix till smooth. Sift flour and baking powder into bowl. Add a little at a time forming a soft dough. Spread in pans with fingers to get into corners. Beat egg whites till stiff. Mix in icing sugar, beat well. Fold in crumbs and almond flavouring. Bake till tooth pick comes out clean.

Peanut Butter Bars

from Pearl Cochrane, Comox, B.C.

Temperature is 350°
Baking time is 30 minutes
Uses a 9x9 inch pan, buttered

Ingredients:

1/2 cup butter or margarine
1/4 cup peanut butter
3/4 cup packed brown sugar
1 egg
1 Tsp. vanilla
2 cups flour
Frosting:
6 oz pkg. semi-sweet choc chips
1/2 cup peanut butter

Method:

Mix all ingredients together in bowl and pack into pan. Bake. Cool.

Frosting:
Melt over low heat semi-sweet chocolate chips, peanut butter and spread on cooled bars.

Scotch Toffee Bars

from Marge Sadler, Tofino, B.C.

Temperature is 400°
Baking time is 12 minutes
Uses a 7 x 11 inch shallow pan, buttered

Ingredients:
- 1/3 cup melted margarine
- 2 cups quick oats
- 1/4 Tsp. salt
- 1/2 cup brown sugar
- 1/4 cup corn syrup
- 1 1/2 Tsp. vanilla
- 1 cup chocolate chips
- 1/2 cup chopped walnuts

Method:
Combine melted margarine and oats. Add salt, sugar, syrup and vanilla. Pack firmly in pan. Be careful not to overbake. Bake 12 minutes. Remove from oven. Sprinkle with chips. Place in oven for about 3 minutes to melt chips. Spread evenly and sprinkle with nuts. Cut immediately. Refrigerate to harden.

Banana Bars

from Rhea Ready, Vancouver, B.C.

Temperature is 350°
Baking time is 25 minutes
Uses a generously buttered 13 x 9 x 2 inch pan

Ingredients:
- 2 large ripe bananas
- 1/2 cup margarine
- 1/2 cup packed brown sugar
- 1/2 cup white sugar
- 1/2 Tsp. cinnamon
- 1/2 Tsp. vanilla
- 1 egg
- 1 cup flour
- 1 Tsp. baking powder
- 1/4 cup chopped nuts

GLAZE:
- 2/3 cup icing sugar
- 1 Tsp. lemon juice
- 2 Tsp. water

Method:
Beat bananas, margarine, sugars, cinnamon and vanilla till well blended. Beat in egg. Mix in flour and baking powder. Then nuts. Spread evenly in pan. Bake. Mix glaze ingredients. Spread on glaze while still hot.

Desperation Squares

from Pearl Cochrane, Comox, B.C.

Temperature is 350°
Baking time is 30 minutes
Uses an 8 x 8 inch pan, buttered

Ingredients:

1/2 cup melted butter or
  margarine
1 cup brown sugar
2 eggs
1 cup flour
1/2 Tsp. salt
1 Tsp. baking powder
1 Tsp. vanilla
1 cup strained crushed
  pineapple
dried fruit, nuts, chips,
  coconut
sugar
cinnamon

Method:

Mix butter, brown sugar, eggs, flour,
salt, baking powder, vanilla all
together. Add 2 cups of dried fruit,
or nuts, or chips, or coconut plus
crushed pineapple. Sprinkle with
sugar and cinnamon before baking
or ice afterwards.

Social Tea Squares

from Alma Cunningham, Victoria, B.C.

Uses a 9x9 inch pan, buttered

Ingredients:

2 beaten eggs
1 cup white sugar
3/4 cup butter
1 Tsp. vanilla
36 crushed tea cookies
5 cups minature coloured
  marshmallows
coconut

Method:

Beat the eggs and sugar together.
Cook on top of stove with butter.
Cool and add vanilla, marshmallows and tea cookies. Place in pan
which has been lined with coconut.
Add coconut to top and set over
night. Cut in squares.

Lemon-Coconut Square

from Gloria Pottage, Victoria, B.C.

Makes 25 squares
Temperature is 350°
Baking time is 20 then 25 minutes
Uses an 8 x 8 inch pan

Ingredients:
BASE:
   1 cup flour
   1/2 cup softened marga-
      rine
   1/4 cup icing sugar
TOPPING:
   2 eggs
   1 cup white sugar
   1/2 Tsp. baking powder
   1/4 Tsp. salt
   2 Tsp. lemon peel
   2 Tbsp. lemon juice
   1/2 cup coconut

Method:
Base: Mix, press into pan and build half inch edges. Bake for 15 - 20 minutes.

Top: Beat till fluffy - 3 minutes. Spread on hot crust. Bake another 20 to 25 minutes. Cool and cut.

Graham Cracker Squares

from Barbara Lenderink, Surrey, B.C.

Temperature is 350°
Baking time is 25 minutes
Uses a 9 x 9 inch pan, buttered

Ingredients:
   20 single graham crackers,
      crumbled
   1 can Eagle Brand milk
   6 oz. chocolate chips

Method:
Mix and put in pan. Bake. Cut when warm. Serve with sprinkled icing sugar on them.

Oatmeal Squares

from Esperanza Kitchen

Temperature is 350°

Ingredients:
- 4 cups oatmeal
- 2 cups brown sugar
- 1/2 Tsp. salt
- 1 cup melted margarine

Method:
Mix oatmeal, brown sugar and salt. Add melted margarine and spread on cookie sheet. Bake until bubbly and soft.

Speculaas
(Dutch Spice Cookies)

from Jackie Vegt, Vancouver, B.C.

Temperature is 350°
Baking time is 30 minutes

Ingredients:
- 3 cups flour
- 1 cup white sugar
- 1 cup brown sugar
- 1 cup butter
- 2 eggs
- 1 Tsp. baking soda
- 2 Tsp. cinnamon
- 1 Tsp. cloves
- 1 Tsp. nutmeg
- 1 Tsp. ginger
- 1 Tsp. allspice

Method:
Mix all together. Press on greased cookie sheet with your hands.

Comment: May use 1 1/2 c. white and 1 1/2 c. whole wheat flour)

Raisin Squares

from Pearl Cochrane, Comox, B.C.

Temperature is 350°
Baking time is 35 - 40 minutes
Uses a 9 x 9 inch pan

Ingredients:

1/2 cup butter or margarine
2/3 cup sugar
1 egg
1 cup raisins
1/2 cup water
1 Tsp. baking soda
1 1/3 cups all purpose flour
1 pinch salt
1 Tsp. vanilla
1/2 Tsp. baking powder

Method:

Cream butter, sugar and egg together. Bring water and raisins to a boil in saucepan. Remove from heat and add baking soda. Cool. Then add creamed mixture. Measure in flour, salt, vanilla and baking powder. Spread in pan. Bake. Sift icing sugar on top when cool if an added touch is required.

Lemon Squares

from Helen Ottom, Campbell River, B.C.

Makes about 4 dozen squares
Temperature is 325°
Baking time is 25 to 30 minutes
Uses an 13 x 9 inch cake pan

Ingredients:

BASE:
2 cups flour
1/2 cup sifted icing sugar
3/4 cup softened butter
FILLING:
2 eggs
1 cup white sugar
1/2 Tsp. baking powder
2 Tsp. lemon peel
2 Tbsp. lemon juice

Method:

Base: Combine flour and icing sugar, stir well. Cut in butter until mixture is crumbly. Press into the pan. Bake for 15 - 20 minutes or until lightly browned.
Filling: Beat eggs, sugar, lemon juice and baking powder until smooth and light. Pour over partially baked crust. Bake for 25 to 30 minutes or until set and golden. Cool. Before serving sprinkle with icing sugar and cut into squares.

Golden Raisin Buns

from Marlene Scott, Campbell River, B.C.

Makes 30 buns
Temperature is 375°
Baking time is 30 - 35 minutes
Uses a cookie sheet

Ingredients:

1 cup water
1/2 cup butter
1 Tsp. sugar
1/4 Tsp. salt
1 cup flour
4 eggs
1/2 cup raisins (optional)

Method:

Bring to boil water, butter, sugar and salt. Add flour all at once. Stir with wooden spoon. Add eggs one at a time. Stir. Add raisins which have been soaking in hot water for 5 minutes. Drop by teaspoonfuls two inches apart on cookie sheet. Bake and then top with a butter icing when cool.

Notes

Candy and Sweets

Chocolate Fudge

from Ruby Quiring, Regina, Sask.

Makes 5 lbs.
Uses three 8 inch or
two 10 inch buttered pans

Ingredients:
1 2/3 cups canned milk
4 1/2 cups granulated
sugar
1 Tsp. salt
32 diced marshmallows
(1/2 lb.)
4 cups semi-sweet choco-
late chips
1 1/2 cups chopped nuts
1 Tsp. vanilla

Method:
Combine milk, sugar and salt in saucepan over medium heat. Heat to boiling point. Cook 5 minutes stirring constantly. Remove from heat. Add marshmallows, chips, vanilla and nuts. Stir 2 minutes (until marshmallows melt). Pour into pans.

Comment:
For me it's a never-fail fudge. This fudge recipe can also be called $500. chocolate fudge. A lady liked a milk company's chocolate fudge so she wrote the company asking for the recipe. The milk company sent the recipe along with a $500. bill. The lady had to pay, so in turn she sent it to all her friends to pass on to others. That's how I got it.

Anise Candy

from Mama Jo Carter, Nebraska

Uses a 9 x 13 inch buttered pan

Ingredients:
2 1/2 cups sugar
3/4 cup white syrup
1 cup water
1/2 Tsp. red food colour-
ing
3/4 Tsp. oil of anise

Method:
Mix sugar, syrup, water and colouring. Put on high heat, boil without stirring to "crack" stage (300°). DO NOT INHALE FUMES WHEN ADDING ANISE. Stir with rubber spatula. Pour into pan. When it starts cooling start cutting!

Home-made Cracker Jacks

from Val Leong, Tahsis. B.C.

Temperature is 350°
Cooking time is 10 - 15 minutes
Uses a cookie sheet

Ingredients:
1/2 cup margarine, melted
1/2 cup corn syrup
1/8 cup molasses
1/4 cup brown sugar
pinch of salt
dash of vanilla
8 cups popped pop corn
1/2 cup peanuts
1 Tsp. sesame seeds

Method:
In pot with medium heat put margarine and corn syrup, molasses and brown sugar. Boil until foamy on top. Add salt and vanilla. Remove from heat. In large bowl put pop corn, peanuts, sesame seeds. Add sauce and toss until well coated. Put on cookie sheet. Bake on middle rack. Shut off oven, leave in awhile too get crunchier. Stir while baking. Recipe can be doubled easily. Can be frozen in heavy plastic bags.Recrisp in oven 5 min. before using.

Almond Roca

from Marlene Scott, Campbell River,B.C.

Ingredients:
2 cups white sugar
1 - 2 cups butter not
margarine
6 oz. bag of chocolate
chips
toasted almonds

Method:
Heat sugar and butter over heat till hard crack stage (310° - 10 to 15 minutes). Pour onto greased cookie sheet. After 2 to 3 minutes spread chocolate chips over top, melt and spread. Sprinkle almonds on top.

63

Marshmallows

from Doris Kreller, Errington, B.C.

Ingredients:
- 2 Tbsp. gelatin
- 4 Tbsp. cold water
- 1/2 cup boiling water
- 1 1/2 cups sugar
- 1/2 Tsp. vanilla
- coconut (optional)
- 1/2 cup icing sugar
  (optional)
- 1 Tbsp. cornstarch
  (optional)

Method:
Soak gelatin in cold water, dissolve in boiling water. When dissolved add sugar and flavouring. After sugar dissolves beat mixture till thick and foaming with electric beater (the more its beaten the better). Pour into a wet mold such as an 8x8 inch pyrex dish rinsed in cold water. Cut into squares and roll in toasted coconut or a mixture of icing sugar and cornstarch.

Almond Crunch Candy

from Eleanor Snyder, Edmonton, Alberta

Uses a 8x8 inch buttered pan

Ingredients:
- 2/3 cup butter
- 1/2 cup honey
- 1 1/2 cups slivered al-
  monds

Method:
Melt butter in heavy skillet. Stir in honey and slivered almonds. Cook over medium heat until mixture turns golden brown. Spread quickly into a buttered pan. Cut into squares while mixture is warm using a buttered knife.

Baked Carmel Corn

from JoAnne Lightbody, New Market, Ont.

Temperature is 225-250°
Baking time is 1 hour
Uses a shallow pan

Ingredients:
1 cup margarine
2 cups brown sugar
1/2 cup white corn syrup
1 Tsp. salt
1 Tsp. vanilla
1/4 Tsp. cream of tartar
1/2 Tsp. baking soda
6 qts. popped corn

Method:
Combine first four ingredients in saucepan and bring to boil. Boil for exactly 5 minutes. Remove from heat and add vanilla, cream of tartar, baking soda. Stir until foamy. Pour over popped corn and mix well. Place in pan and bake in oven stirring every 15 minutes. Remove from oven. Cool and break apart. Store in tightly covered container.

Nuts & Bolts

from Esperanza Kitchen

Temperature is 200°
Baking time is 2 hours
Uses a cookie sheet

Ingredients:
1 box Shreddies
1 box pretzel sticks
1 box Cheerios
1 1/2 lb. peanuts
1 cup butter, melted
1 cup margarine, melted
2 Tsp. Worcestershire sauce
1 Tsp. celery salt
1 Tsp. garlic salt
1 Tsp. onion salt

Method:
Combine all ingredients and mix thoroughly. Place on cookie sheet. Bake. Cover for the first half hour. Open for the last 1 1/2 hours.

Notes

Canning

Green Tomato Pickles

from Alma Cunningham, Victoria, B.C.

Ingredients:
20 large green tomatoes
5 cups white sugar
1 1/2 Tsp. allspice
1 Tsp. tumeric
8 onions (4 is enough)
4 cups vinegar or less
1 Tsp. cinnamon
2 Tsp. black pepper
2 Tsp. salt

Method:
Slice tomatoes and onions. Leave in bowl overnight. In morning drain. Add other ingredients. Put into saucepan. Bring to gentle boil. Simmer for one hour. Put in sterilized jars - will seal from own heat.

Salsa Sauce

from Coastal Missions, Chemainus, B.C.

Microwave

Ingredients:
1 - 16 oz. can chopped tomatoes
1 - 4 oz. can chopped chili peppers
or fresh peppers (Jalapenos)
1/2 cup chopped onion
1 Tbsp. vinegar
1 Tsp. sugar
1/4 Tsp. salt

Method:
Place in microwave safe casserole dish. Microwave for 20 minutes at Power 5. Stir after 10 minutes. Cover with plastic wrap - leave air space.

Blackberry Syrup

from Judy Ellis, Tahsis, B.C.

Ingredients:
- 3 1/2 cups berry juice
- 3 1/2 cups white sugar
- 1 1/2 cups white corn syrup

Method:
Combine ingredients in large saucepan. Bring to a rolling boil. Stir constantly. Pour hot juice into jars. Seal. If the natural pectin jells it in storage, warm it to a pourable consistency.

Note: Sterilize jars and if you have a steam juice extractor this recipe works well with salal berries.

Apple Green Tomato Mincemeat

from Betty Rashleigh, Sidney, B.C.

Ingredients:
- 15 apples not peeled
- 20 green tomatoes
- 8 red peppers (optional)
- 5 cups brown sugar
- 1 Tbsp. pepper
- 1 Tbsp. coarse salt
- 1 Tsp. cloves
- 4 cups vinegar (no water)

Method:
Cut up or grind with coarse grinder vegetables and apples. Add to vinegar the spices and sugar. Be sure vinegar, etc. is boiling before vegetables are added to it. Boil the combined mixture for 30 minutes. Put in hot jars and seal with wax.

Jelly Making

from Edith Gibson, Victoria, B.C.

Ingredients:
- 1 Tsp. Epsom salts
- 6 cups fruit juice

Method:
Use one teaspoon of Epsom salts instead of Certo to 6 cups of fruit juice when making jelly.

Rhubarb & Strawberry Jam

from Cy Lazell, Victoria, B.C.

Ingredients:
- 3 cups rhubarb, sliced fine
- 2 cups crushed strawberries
- 4 cups sugar
- 1 small pkg. strawberry jello

Method:
To make a smooth jam add 1 or 2 Tbsp. of water to rhubarb. Cover pan and gently cook over low heat till it becomes soft. Check it often so it doesn't stick and burn on bottom. Add strawberries. Stir and gently cook or heat up well. Add sugar, stir and boil till it thickens. Add jello and stir until well dissolved. Pour into **sterilized** jars.

Comment: Jam needs constant watching so it doesn't stick and burn. The recipe says to boil 30 minutes but it may not take that long. When it gets a thick look and forms a rounded drop or sheets from the edge of the spoon, it is done. You can make many half and half mixtures with rhubarb. The general rule with jam is to measure the cooked fruit and add cup for cup of sugar. To lesson the boiling time Certo crystals can be added. Recipes are enclosed with package.

Note: Sterilize jars first

Apple Cider Jelly

from Hilda McPherson, Meaford, Ontario

Ingredients:
- 4 cups cider
- 5 cups sugar
- 2 Tbsp. red cinnamon candies
- 1 pkg. sure jell

Method:
Bring cider, candies and sure jell to a boil. Add sugar. Bring to a full boil and boil for 1 minute. Pour in jars and seal.

Note: Sterilize jars first

Strawberry Preserves

from Hilda McPherson, Meaford, Ontario

Ingredients:
- 2 quarts strawberries
- boiling water
- 6 cups sugar

Method:
Scald strawberries in boiling water for two minutes. Drain. Add 4 cups sugar. Gently toss. Bring to boil and boil 2 minutes. Counting time after full contents is bubbling. Remove from stove until bubbling stops. Add 2 more cups of sugar. Boil again for 5 minutes. Counting as before. Pour into shallow pan so that preserves are not more than 1 1/2 - 2 inches deep. Let stand overnight. In morning put in sterile jars, seal. Berries will be red and plump.

Note: Sterilize jars first

Beet Relish

from Alma Cunningham, Victoria, B.C.

Ingredients:
- 12 medium beets
- 8 onions
- 3 red sweet peppers
- 3 green sweet peppers
- 3 cups sugar
- 3 Tsp. salt
- 1 quart vinegar

Method:
Cook beets till done. Then peel and grind through chopper. Then grind peppers and onions. Put vinegar, salt and sugar on stove. Add beets, onions, peppers and cook until done. Seal.

Note: Sterilize jars first

Mincemeat

from Audrey Barnett, Port Coquitlam, B.C.

Cooking time is 1 1/2 hours

Ingredients:
- 1 lb. ground beef
- 1 lb. raisins
- 1 lb. currants
- 1/2 lb. mixed peel
- 1 can cherries, pitted with juice
- 5 cups (or more) chopped apples
- 1 - 40 oz. can grapefruit juice
- 1/3 cup vinegar
- 2 cups brown sugar
- 1 Tbsp. ginger
- 1 Tbsp. allspice
- 1 Tbsp. cinnamon

Method:
Combine and simmer. Put into hot sealers. (I let it cook longer because I like the smell of it cooking.)

Note: Best if made 4-6 weeks before needed so it can age.

Green Tomato Relish

from Martha Holm, Powell River, B.C.

Ingredients:
- 6 quarts green tomatoes
- 6 large onions
- 2 green peppers
- 2 sweet red peppers
- 5 Tsp. salt
- 5 Tsp. curry powder
- 6 Tsp. celery seed
- 3 cups vinegar
- 4 cups white sugar

Method:
Put tomatoes through food chopper and cook for 20 minutes. Drain. Add chopped onions, vinegar, sugar and spices. Cook 20 minutes. Then add peppers. Cook 10 minutes more. Seal. (Good when we have hamburgers.)

Note: Sterilize jars first

Green Tomato Mincemeat

from Martha Holm, Powell River, B.C.

Ingredients:
- 2 1/2 cups chopped green tomatoes
- 3 3/4 cups chopped tart apples
- 3 cups sugar
- 2 Tsp. cinnamon
- 1/4 cup vinegar
- 3 cups raisins
- 1 Tsp. salt
- 1 Tsp. allspice
- 1 Tsp. cloves

Method:
Mix all ingredients together. Place in large saucepan and bring quickly to a boil. Lower heat and simmer until thick, stirring occasionaly. Pour into jars. Seal. (This is even better than store-bought mincemeat.)

Note: Sterilize jars first

Notes

Desserts

Cheese Cake

from Marlene Scott, Campbell River, B.C.

Temperature is 350°
Baking time is 10 minutes
Uses a 9 inch pie or square pan

Ingredients:

CRUST:
  1 1/2 cups graham crumbs
  1/4 cup melted butter
  1/4 cup icing sugar

FILLING:
  3 oz. pkg. lemon jello
  1 cup boiling water
  8 oz. pkg. cream cheese
  whipping cream (small)
  1/2 cup sugar
  crushed pineapple, small tin
  1/2 container sour cream

Method:

Combine crust ingredients and pat into pan. Bake. Cool. Dissolve lemon jello in boiling water. Set in fridge. Beat together cream cheese and whipping cream. Whip chilled jello with sugar. Pour onto baked graham crust. Top with combined pineapple and sour cream.

Harris' Favourite Cheese Cake

from Lou Harris, Union Bay, B.C.

Temperature is 350 - 400°
Baking time is Various
Uses a pie pan

Ingredients:

CRUST:
  1/4 lb. margarine, melted
  1 1/2 cups graham crumbs
  1/8 cup frosting sugar

FILLING:
  2 eggs, beaten
  12 oz. cream cheese
  1/2 cup granulated sugar
  1/2 Tsp. vanilla

TOPPING:
  1/2 pint sour cream
  1/2 cup granulated sugar
  1/2 Tsp. vanilla

Method:

Combine crust ingredients and pat into pie and bake for 10 minutes at 350°. Combine filling ingredients and beat till creamy. Pour into baked crust. Bake 20 minutes at 350°. Remove from oven and cool 20 minutes. Combine topping ingredients and beat. Pour over cooled pie. Bake 5 minutes at 475°. Remove from oven and cool. Allow two hours (at least) before serving. Store in fridge.

No-Bake Lemon Cheese Cake

from Myrna Hill, M/V Anastasis

Uses 3 - 9 inch pie pans

Ingredients:
CRUMB CRUST:
- 2 cups graham crumbs
- 2 Tbsp. hot water
- 1/2 cup melted butter
- 1/2 cup brown sugar (optional)

FILLING:
- 1 small pkt. lemon jello
- 3/4 cup boiling water
- 2 Tsp. grated lemon rind
- 1/4 cup lemon juice
- 1 15oz. tin evaporated milk
- 8 oz. cream cheese
- 1 cup icing sugar
- 1 Tsp. vanilla

Method:
Combine crumbs, butter and 2 Tbsp. hot water. Press into pie pans. Chill. For the filling dissolve jelly crystals in boiling water. Add lemon rind and juice. Cool slightly. Beat chilled milk till thick. Beat cream cheese till smooth. Add sugar, vanilla and milk. Beat again. Fold in jelly mixture. Pour into chilled crumb crusts and chill for several hours. Decorate as desired.

No Bake Cheese Cake

from Kay MacBeth, Comox, B.C.

Temperature is 350°
Baking time is 7 minutes
Uses a 9 inch pan or pie plate

Ingredients:
CRUST
- 1 1/2 cups graham crumbs
- 1/4 cup melted butter
- 1/4 cup icing sugar

FILLING:
- 8 oz. cream cheese
- 1 1/2 cups icing sugar
- 2 oz. pkg. dream whip
- cherry pie filling

Method:
Combine crust ingredients and put in pan 1/4 inch thick. Bake 7 minutes. Cool. Cream together cream cheese and icing sugar and fold in dream whip. Put on top of crumbs. Spread over top cherry pie filling.

Banana Split Cake

from Beatrice Sam, Tofino, B.C.

Makes 12 servings

Ingredients:
2 cups cookie crumb mix
1/4 cup melted margarine
2 eggs
1 cup butter or margarine
softened
2 cups sifted powdered
sugar
3 - 4 bananas
1 15 oz can crushed/
drained pineapple
1 13 oz whipped topping
thawed*
or 1 pt. sweetened
whipped cream
1/4 to 1/2 cup chopped
nuts

Method:
In a medium bowl combine cookie crumb crust mix. Add 1/4 cup melted margarine. Press into pan. In a medium bowl combine eggs, 1 cup butter, powdered sugar.Beat till smooth,10-15 min.Spread over crust.Refrigerate 3-4 hrs.Just before serving slice bananas over mixture.Add drained pineapple evenly over bananas. Top with whipped topping or whipped cream. Sprinkle with nuts.

*COOL WHIP CAN BE USED.

Cookie Crumb Crust Mix

from Beatrice Sam, Tofino, B.C.

Makes 10 cups of mix
Temperature is 375°
Baking time is 15 minutes
Uses a shallow baking pan

Ingredients:
6 cups all purpose flour
1 1/2 cups chopped nuts
1 1/2 cups firmly packed
brown sugar
1 lb. butter or marg,
softened

Method:
With a pastry blender cut in butter or margarine until mixture resembles cornmeal in texture. Press mixture firmly into two unbuttered shallow baking pans. Bake. Cool. Crumble and store in a large airtight container. Label. Use within 4 - 6 weeks.

Mocha Roll for Blender

from Airie Kirby, Campbell River, B.C.

Makes 10 servings
Temperature is 400°
Baking time is 8 - 10 minutes
Uses a 15x10x1 inch pan, buttered

Ingredients:

4 eggs
1/2 Tsp. salt
3/4 cup sugar
1 Tsp. vanilla
3/4 cup regular pancake
  mix
1 1/2 cups milk
1 - 4 serving size chocolate
  pudding mix
1 Tbsp. instant coffee
icing sugar
shaved chocolate bar bits
whipping cream
  (optional)

Method:

Blend eggs, salt till frothy. Add sugar, vanilla. Blend till smooth and thick. Add pancake mix. Blend to combine. Spread batter onto pan. Bake. Immediately loosen sides. Turn onto towel dusted with icing sugar. Start with narrow end and roll cake and towel together. Cool. Place milk, pudding, coffee into blender till combined. Unroll cooled cake. Spread with mixture. Reroll. Chill. When ready top with sifted icing sugar, shaved chocolate or whipped cream.

Blueberry Dessert

from Beatrice Sam, Tofino, B.C.

Makes 15 - 20 servings
Uses an 11 x 17 inch pan

Ingredients:

3 cups cookie crumb mix
  on p. 78
2 eggs
1 cup butter or margarine
2 cups powdered sugar
2 - 3oz pkg. cream cheese
1 - 21 oz can blueberry pie
  filling
1 cup whipped cream,
  whipped
1/2 cup chopped nuts

Method:

Press 2 cups cookie crumb mix onto the bottom of pan. In medium bowl cream together eggs, butter or margarine, powdered sugar and cream cheese until smooth. Spread over crumb layer. Spread blueberry pie filling evenly over top. Refrigerate for at least 12 hours. Just before serving top with whipped cream and sprinkle with a mixture of 1 cup cookie crumbs and pecans. Cut into squares.

Tammy's New Zealand Pavlova

from Tammy Hill, M/V Anastasis

Temperature is 375°
Cooking time is 40 - 50 minutes
Uses a slightly buttered cookie sheet

Ingredients:
6 eggs
2 cups sugar
2 Tbsp. cornstarch
2 Tsp. vinegar
1 Tsp. vanilla
whipped cream
fresh or canned fruit

Method:
Beat first five ingredients lots and lots - till very thick. Put on cookie sheet in a 9 - 10 inch circle. Bake. To serve: top with generous amount of whipped cream artistically decorated with fruit. To make it authentically New Zealand, top with sweet and juicy green Kiwi fruit.

Pineapple Slice

from Kay Good, Coquitlam, B.C.

Temperature is 350°
Baking time is 20 minutes
Uses a 9x12 inch pan

Ingredients:
BASE:
2 cups flour
1 cup margarine
2 Tbsp. sugar
pinch of salt
FILLING:
2 Tbsp. cornstarch
1/4 cup granulated sugar
1 15oz can pineapple
crushed/undrained
1/4 cup cold water
3/4 cup chopped
maraschino cherries
TOPPING:
2 egg whites
2 Tbsp. sugar
Almond flavouring
Sprinkle of coconut

Method:
Combine base ingredients and pat into pan. Bake. Combine water and cornstarch and mix well. Then add remaining filling ingredients. Cook on top of stove till thickened. Pour over base. Combine egg whites and sugar and flavouring to form meringue. Spoon over dessert and brown in oven.

Almond Puff

from Lois Hooks, Edmonton, Alberta

Temperature is 350°
Baking time is 60 minutes
Uses a Cookie sheet

Ingredients:
BASE:
- 1/2 cup soft margarine
- 1 cup flour
- 2 Tbsp. water
- 1/2 cup margarine
- 1 cup water
- 1 Tsp. almond extract
- 1 cup flour
- 3 eggs

GLAZE:
- 1 1/2 cups icing sugar
- 2 Tbsp. margarine
- 1 Tsp. almond extract
- 1 - 2 Tbsp. warm water

Method:
Cut 1/2 cup margarine into 1 cup flour. Sprinkle 2 Tbsp. water over and mix with fork. Form into ball, divide in half. On cookie sheet pat each half into 12x3 strip, about 3 inches apart. In saucepan heat margarine, 1 cup water to rolling boil. Remove. Stir in almond extract, 1 cup flour. Stir vigorously over low heat until mixture forms ball - 1 min. Remove. Beat in eggs 1 at a time. Divide in half. Spread over strips, covering completely. Bake, cool, glaze.

Peppermint Dream Dessert

from Marion McLean

Uses a 9 x 13 inch loaf pan

Ingredients:
- 2 pkgs. Oreo chocolate cookies
- 1/4 cup melted butter
- 30 large marshmallows
- 1/2 cup milk
- 1/2 Tsp. peppermint flavouring
- green food colouring
- 1 1/2 cups whpping cream

Method:
Crunch cookies and moisten with melted butter. Use 2/3 cup of crumbs to line bottom of pan. Heat marshmallows and milk in double boiler until dissolved. Add peppermint and a few drops of food colouring. Cool. Whip up cream. Fold into marshmallow mixture. Put on top of crumbs and sprinkle remaining crumbs on top of cream filling. Refrigerate until used.

Pumpkin Roll

from Ginger Cleveland, California

Temperature is 350°
Baking time is 10 - 12 minutes
Uses a cookie sheet lined with buttered wax paper

Ingredients:

3 eggs
1 cup sugar
2/3 cup canned
pumpkin(not premixed)
1 Tsp. baking soda
1 Tsp. cinnamon
3/4 cup flour
3/4 cup chopped nuts (if
desired)
FILLING:
1 - 8oz. pkg. softened
cream cheese
2 Tbsp. margarine
1 cup powdered sugar
1 Tsp. vanilla

Method:

Mix top 7 ingredients together in large bowl. Pour out batter onto wax paper. Smooth out until even. Do not touch edges with batter. Bake. Turn cake onto lightly powdered sugar wax paper. Peel off wax paper and then roll up cake in wax paper and let set until cool. Unroll. Mix filling and spread on cake. Re-roll (without wax paper) after filling is spread out evenly on cake. Wrap in foil and refrigerate.

Pineapple Loaf

from Beulah Harnum, Vancouver, B.C.

Serves 8
Uses a loaf pan

Ingredients:

1 cup crushed/drained
pineapple
2 envelopes gelatin
1/2 cup pineapple juice
1/4 cup sugar
2 Tbsp. lemon juice
pinch salt
3 eggs, separated
1 1/2 cups tin milk
1/4 cup sugar

Method:

Soften gelatin in pineapple juice. In double boiler put sugar, 3 egg yolks, milk. Cook till liquid sticks to spoon. Remove. Add gelatin, pineapple and lemon juice. Put in fridge until cool. Beat egg whites. Add 1/4 cup of sugar and salt. Fold in first mix. Rinse loaf pan in cold water. Pour mixture in. When set tip out and cover with dream whip or whipped cream.

Special Dessert

from Lorna Penner, Kyuquot, B.C.

Temperature is 325°
Baking time is 7 minutes
Uses an 8 x 8 inch pan

Ingredients:
- 7 double graham wafers
- 1/4 cup butter
- 1/8 cup brown sugar
- 1 pkg. strawberry whip & chill
- 1 cup whipping cream
- 1/2 cup white sugar
- 1/2 pkg. minature marsh-mallows
- 1 pkg. frozen berries

Method:
Mix graham wafer crumbs, butter and sugar. Put in pan and bake. Cool. Mix whip and chill according to package. Put on crumb base. Whip cream, add sugar, mix in marshmallows and partially thawed berries. Mix. Pour this over whip and chill base. Sprinkle small amount of strawberry jello powder over cream mixture. Chill in fridge for 24 hours. Cut in squares and serve.

Note: You can use strawberries or raspberries.

Fruit Cocktail Cake

from Esperanza Kitchen

Temperature is 350°
Baking time is 45 - 50 minutes
Uses an 8 x 8 inch greased pan

Ingredients:
- 1 cup flour
- 1/2 cup sugar
- 1 Tsp. baking powder
- 16 oz. drained fruit cocktail
- 1 egg
- 2 Tbsp. margarine
- 2 Tbsp. brown sugar

Method:
Combine flour, sugar and baking powder. Stir in until flour is moist the fruit cocktail, egg and margarine. Put in pan. Sprinkle with brown sugar. Bake.

Krispie Ice-Cream Squares

from Dot McPherson, Whitby, Ont.

Ingredients:
- 5 cups rice krispies
- 1 scant cup melted butter
- 1 cup coconut
- 1/2 cup brown sugar
- ice cream

Method:
Mix rice krispies, butter, coconut and brown sugar together. Pat half of this mixture into pan. Cover with softened ice cream. Cover with remaining crumbs. Chill.

Dutch Apple Square

from Audrey Dol, Tahsis, B.C.

Temperature is 350°
Cooking time is 30 - 40 minutes

Ingredients:
- 1 cup margarine
- 1 cup sugar
- 1 egg
- 2 cups flour
- 1 Tsp. baking powder
- 3 - 4 large apples
- 4 Tbsp. sugar
- Cinnamon to taste

Method:
Mix first five ingredients together. Make dough into a ball, press 2/3 of the ball into a 9x13 inch buttered pan. Arrange sliced apples onto this, sprinkle with sugar and cinnamon. Pinch off pieces of remaining dough, flatten in your hands and arrange over apple slices. Bake.

Pineapple Delight

from Glenna Smuland, Kelowna, B.C.

Ingredients:
- 1 can crushed pineapple
- 1 cup sugar
- 1 Tbsp. flour
- 2 eggs, beaten
- 1 Tbsp. butter
- 1 cup whipped cream
- 2 or 3 bananas

Method:
Drain juice from pineapple. To the juice add sugar, flour and eggs. Cook in double boiler till thickened. When cool mix in whipped cream or 1 envelope of Dream Whip - whipped and drained pineapple and bananas. Makes a large pudding.

84

Apple Crunch

from Colleen Shonwise, Tahsis, B.C.

Temperature is 350°
Baking time is 60 minutes
Uses a 9 x 9 inch pan, buttered

Ingredients:
- 1 cup flour
- 3/4 cup oatmeal
- 1 cup brown sugar
- 1 Tsp. cinnamon
- 1/2 cup butter
- 4 cups chopped or sliced apples (rhubarb)
- 1 cup sugar
- 2 Tbsp. cornstarch
- 1 cup water
- 1 Tsp. vanilla

Method:
Mix flour, oatmeal, brown sugar, cinnamon and melted butter until crumbly. Press into pan, saving 2/3 cup for topping. Cover with apples. Combine sugar, cornstarch, water, vanilla and cook until clear and thick. Pour over fruit. Top with remaining crumbs. Bake.

Pumpkin Dessert

from Glenna Smuland, Kelowna, B.C.

Temperature is 350°
Baking time is 1 hour
Uses a 9 x 13 greased pan

Ingredients:
- 4 beaten eggs
- 28 oz. can of pumpkin
- 1 1/2 cups sugar
- 2 Tsp. cinnamon
- 1 Tsp. ginger
- 1/2 Tsp. flour
- 1 - 14 oz. can milk
- 1 yellow cake mix
- 3/4 cup margarine
- 1/2 cup walnuts

Method:
Combine ingredients and pour into pan. Top with 1 yellow cake mix and 3/4 cup margarine. Sprinkle on mixture. Bake for 30 minutes. Sprinkle on 1/2 cup walnuts. Bake for 30 minutes more.

Rice Pudding

from Esperanza Kitchen

Makes 12 - 15 servings
Temperature is 275°
Baking time is 2 1/2 hours
Uses a casserole or roasting pan

Ingredients:
- 1/2 cup rice
- 1/2 cup sugar
- 1/4 cup margarine
- 1/2 Tsp. salt
- 1/4 Tsp. nutmeg
- 1/2 cup raisins
- 8 cups cold milk

Method:
Mix all ingredients into dish. Bake uncovered stirring every half hour. (It may look runny when taken out of the oven but it will set as it cools.)

Danish Christmas Rice Pudding

from Hanne Reid, Steinback, Man.

Serves 4

Ingredients:
- 1 3/4 cups milk
- 1/2 cup pearl or dessert rice
- 1/8 cup sugar
- 1 Tsp. vanilla
- 1 envelope gelatin
- 1/4 cup almonds, chopped
- 1 1/4 cups whipping cream
- 1 can cherries
- 1 Tbsp. cornstarch

Method:
Bring milk to boil. Sprinkle over rice. Simmer 15 minutes, stirring often. Prepare gelatin according to packet instructions. Add to rice along with sugar and vanilla. Place in fridge till its thickened and cool. Whip cream and fold rice and almonds in. Chill. To serve let pudding sit at room temperature. Prepare cherry sauce - mix can of cherries with cornstarch. Bring to boil. Stir until clear & thick. Serve warm over pudding

Quick Pudding

from Esperanza Kitchen

Temperature is 375°
Baking time is 45 minutes
Uses a 2 Quart Casserole dish

Ingredients:
1 cup flour
1/2 cup brown sugar
2 Tsp. baking powder
1 cup raisins
1/4 Tsp. salt
1/2 cup milk
1 cup brown sugar
3 cups boiling water
1 Tbsp. butter

Method:
Mix together first six ingredients and place in baking dish. Then combine the next three ingredients and pour over batter. Bake in hot oven.

Hot Fudge Pudding

from Sharon Gerber, Alix, Alberta

Temperature is 350°
Baking time is 45 minutes
Uses a 9 x 9 inch pan

Ingredients:
1 cup flour
2 Tsp. baking powder
1/4 Tsp. salt
3/4 cup sugar
2 Tbsp. cocoa
1/2 cup milk
2 Tbsp. melted shortening
1 cup chopped nuts
TOPPING:
1 cup brown sugar
1/4 cup cocoa
1 3/4 cups hot water

Method:
Mix first five ingredients. Add milk, shortening, nuts and spread in pan. Sprinkle with brown sugar and cocoa mixture. Pour hot water over. Bake.

Carrot Pudding

from Pearl Cochrane, Comox, B.C.

Ingredients:

1 cup grated raw carrots
1 cup grated raw potato
1 cup grated raw apple
1 1/2 cups sifted all purpose flour
1 Tsp. salt
1 Tsp. cinnamon
1 Tsp. allspice
1 Tsp. nutmeg
3/4 cup white sugar
1 cup grated suet or 1/2
cup butter
1 1/2 cups raisins
1/2 cup chopped nuts

Method:

Combine grated carrots, potatoes
and apples together. Sift flour, salt,
soda, spices and sugar. Add suet or
butter. Combine all ingredients and
turn into well-greased mold filling
not more than 2/3 full. Cover with
wax paper, then foil and tie
down.Steam 3 hours on closed
covered steamer. Serve hot with
your favourite sauce.

Berry Cake

from Sylvia Hammond, Victoria, B.C.

Temperature is 350°
Baking time is 40 - 50 minutes
Uses a 9 x 13 inch pan, buttered

Ingredients:

2 or 3 eggs
1 cup milk
1 1/4 cups sugar
2 cups flour
1 Tbsp. baking powder
1/2 Tsp. salt
1/4 cup oil or melted
margarine
3 cups berries (raspberry,
etc.)

Method:

Beat eggs, 3/4 cup sugar and milk.
Sift dry ingredients and add to wet.
Add oil. Put batter into pan. Spread
your choice of the berries over batter
and sprinkle with remaining 1/2
cup sugar. Bake. Cool on rack for
about 10 minutes. Then cut and
serve or finish cooling out of pan.
Can be frozen.

Apple - Apricot Cake

from Jackie Vegt, Vancouver, B.C.

Temperature is 350°
Baking time is 45 minutes
Uses a cookie sheet
lined with greased wax paper

Ingredients:
6 eggs
1 1/2 cups butter or margarine
1 1/2 cups sugar
1 3/4 cups flour
1 Tsp. baking powder
1 Tsp. salt
6 apples
lemon juice
1 can apriocots (or peaches)

Method:
Cream butter and the sugar. Beat in one egg at a time. Add dry ingredients, beat. Spread batter on cookie sheet. Peal apples, core and slice into a bowl. Cover apples with a few tablespoons lemon juice. Place apple slices in rows on batter. Bake. Heat canned fruit in a saucepan. Thicken with about two tablespoons corn starch. Spread fruit onto golden baked batter and apples. Cut into squares and serve when chilled.

Apple Pudding Cake

from Colleen Shonwise, Tahsis, B.C.

Temperature is 350°
Baking time is 40 - 45 minutes
Uses a greased 8 x 8 inch square pan

Ingredients:
5 Tbsp. soft butter or margarine
1 cup sugar
1 beaten egg
3 cups of dried apples
1/2 cup walnuts
1 Tsp. vanilla
1 cup flour
1 Tsp. baking soda
1/2 Tsp. salt
1/4 Tsp. nutmeg
1/2 Tsp. cinnamon

Method:
Cream butter and sugar add egg and mix well. Stir in apples, walnuts and vanilla. Mix flour, baking soda, salt, nutmeg and cinnamon. Stir in dry ingredients just until there is no traces of flour. Pour into the pan and bake.

Easy Chocolate Eclair Cake

from Dottie Dale, Seattle, Wash.

Uses a 8 inch buttered pan

Ingredients:

- 45 graham crackers
- 2 sm. pk. instant vanilla pudding
- 3 cups milk
- 1 (8 or 9 oz) cool whip

TOPPING

- 2 squares melted chocolate
- 1 1/2 cups powdered sugar
- 1 Tsp. vanilla
- 3 Tbsp. milk
- 3 Tbsp. white KARO syrup
- 2 Tbsp. softened margarine

Method:

Line bottom of pan with 15 crackers. Mix pudding with milk until thick. Fold in cool whip. Spread half of mixture over crackers. Add 15 more crackers. Spread with remaining pudding. Add 15 more crackers. Mix topping ingredients together until smooth and spread over top layer of graham crackers. Refrigerate overnight.

Notes

Pies

Pie Crust

from Dottie Dale, Seattle, Wash.

makes 4 crusts

Ingredients:
- 3 cups flour
- 1 Tsp. salt
- 1 1/4 cups Crisco
- 1 egg
- 1 Tbsp. vinegar
- 5 Tbsp. water

Method:
Combine flour and salt. Cut in Crisco. Combine in separate bowl the egg, vinegar and water. Mix well. Stir into flour-shortening mixture.

Never Fail Pastry

from Dorthea McLean, Surrey, B.C.

Ingredients:
- 5 cups flour
- 1 Tsp. salt
- 1 Tsp. baking powder
- 3 Tbsp. brown sugar
- 1 lb. shortening
- 1 beaten egg
- 2 Tbsp. vinegar
- water

Method:
Mix dry ingredients well. Add shortening (half at a time). Put in measuring cup beaten egg, vinegar and enough water to make one cup. Pour full amount of liquid into dry ingredients and shortening mix. Mix with hands until you can form into oblong roll (8 inches approx.). Cut into 4 equal parts. Each part makes 2 bottom shells or 1 top and 1 bottom or 8 tart shells.

Best Butter Tarts

from Dot McPherson, Whitby, Ont.

Temperature is 400°
Baking time is 10 - 15 minutes
Uses muffin or tart tins

Ingredients:
1 cup butter
3 cups brown sugar
1 cup raisins
4 large eggs
4 Tbsp. 18% cream
4 Tsp. vanilla
1 cup chopped pecans
pastry

Method:
Melt butter and sugar over low heat. Add raisins, let cool. Beat eggs, cream, vanilla. Stir in nuts and sugar mixture. Line tart tins with pastry and fill 2/3 full. Bake

Butter Tart Filling

from Audrey Lore, NewWestminster, B.C.

Temperature is 400°
Baking time is 10 - 15 minutes
Uses a muffin or tart tins

Ingredients:
1 cup raisins or currants
1 cup brown sugar (scant)
1 egg
1 Tsp. lemon juice and
  rind
1/2 Tsp. vanilla
1/2 Tsp. nutmeg
  (optional, good)
2 Tbsp. butter

Method:
Melt butter and sugar over low heat. Add raisins and let cool. Beat eggs, lemon juice and rind, vanilla, nutmeg and stir into sugar mixture. Line tart tins with pastry and fill 2/3 full. Bake.

Impossible Coconut Pie

from Dorthea McLean, Surrey, B.C.

Temperature is 350°F
Baking time is 60 minutes

Ingredients:
4 eggs
1/2 cup butter
1/2 cup flour
2 cups milk
1 cup sugar
1 cup coconut
2 Tsp. vanilla
pinch of salt

Method:
Blend together above ingredients in blender or beat. Pour into pie plate (preferably glass). Bake until centre is firm and top is golden brown.

Ritz Cracker Apple Pie (No Apples!)

from Helena McMann, Gold River, B.C.

Temperature is 425°
Baking time is 30 - 35 minutes

Ingredients:
Pastry for two crust pie
2 cups water
1 1/4 cups sugar
2 Tsp. cream of tarter
1 Tsp. cinnamon
1/4 Tsp. nutmeg
butter or margarine
20 ritz crackers

Method:
Combine water, sugar, cream of tartar. Bring to boil. Drop ritz crackers whole into mixture and keep boiling until transparent. About 8 - 10 minutes. Pour mixture into baked pie crust. Sprinkle with cinnamon and nutmeg. Dot with butter. Cover with top crust, trim and flute edges together. Cut slits in top to let steam escape. Bake in hot oven. Serve warm.

Banana Pie

from Alma Cunningham, Victoria, B.C.

Ingredients:
- Baked single pie shell
- 2 bananas
- 1 cup milk
- 1/2 cup sugar
- 2 egg yolks
- 2 Tbsp. flour
- 2 egg whites
- 1 Tbsp. white sugar

Method:

Slice two bananas into pie shell. Put milk, sugar, egg yolks, and flour in double boiler and cook until thick. Let cool and pour over bananas. Beat egg whites and sugar and spread over top of pie. Brown meringue in oven.

Butterscotch Pie

from Donna Paracy, Tahsis, B.C.

Ingredients:
- Single baked pie shell
- 2 egg yolks, beaten
- 2 Tbsp. cornstarch
- 2 Tbsp. flour
- 1/2 Tsp. salt
- 2 cups milk
- 3/4 cup brown sugar
- 2 Tbsp. butter
- 1 - 2 Tsp. vanilla

Method:

Mix together with part of the two cups of milk the egg yolks, flour, cornstarch and salt. Add remaining milk, bring to boil. Add brown sugar, butter and vanilla. Blend and pour into pie shell.

Apple Cream Pie

from Kathy Harmsworth, Esperanza, B.C.

Ingredients:
Single pie shell, unbaked
2 cups finely chopped tart
   apples
3/4 cup sugar
2 Tbsp. flour
1 cup sour cream
1 egg, beaten
1/2 Tsp. vanilla
1/8 Tsp. salt
TOPPING:
1/3 cup sugar
1 Tsp. cinnamon
1/3 cup flour
1/4 cup butter

Method:
Combine sugar and flour. Add cream, egg, flavouring and salt. Beat until smooth. Add apples. Mix well. Pour into unbaked pie shell. Bake in 450° oven for 15 minutes. Reduce to 325° and bake for 30 minutes. Combine sugar, cinnamon, flour and butter and sprinkle over pie. Bake 325° for 20 minutes.

Rhubarb Pie

from Dottie Dale, Seattle, Wash.

Temperature is 400 - 350°
Baking time is 10 - 40 minutes

Ingredients:
Double pie crust
4 heaping cups rhubarb,
   sliced thin
boiling water
1 1/2 cups sugar
1/4 cup flour
1/2 Tsp. salt
2 eggs beaten slightly

Method:
Pour boiling water over rhubarb. Let stand a few minutes. Drain well. Combine sugar, flour, salt and eggs. Mix together well. Stir into drained rhubarb. Spoon into unbaked pie crust. Top with second crust. Bake at 400° for 10 minutes then turn oven down to 350° for 40 minutes.

Poor Man's Pecan Pie

from Rhea Ready, Vancouver, B.C.

Temperature is 350°
Baking time is 60 minutes
Uses a 9 inch pie pan

Ingredients:
single unbaked pie shell
1 cup uncooked oatmeal
1 cup brown sugar
1 cup dark corn syrup
1/2 cup melted margarine
2 eggs

Method:
Mix together in bowl above ingredients and pour into pie shell. Bake. Delicious served with whipped cream.

Pumpkin Chiffon Pie

from Ruby Quiring, Regina, Sask.

Serves 6 - 8

Ingredients:
CRUST:
1/4 - 1/3 cup melted margarine
1 1/2 cups graham crumbs
FILLING:
2 cups or 16 oz. cooked pumpkin
1 cup skim milk
1 Tsp. cinnamon
1/2 Tsp. ginger
1/2 Tsp. nutmeg
3/4 Tsp. salt
1/2 cup sugar or powdered Equal
2 pkgs. Knox gelatin
1/2 cup cold water
4 Tbsp. boiling water

Method:
Mix crust ingredients and pat into pie plate. Set in fridge for 10 min. Pour cold water over gelatin, set aside. In blender put pumpkin, milk, spices, salt, sugar. Add boiling water to gelatin. Stir. Add to pumpkin mixture. Blend well. Pour into graham crust. Refrigerate till it sets. (Saran Wrap prevents a hard crust from forming.) Serve with whipped cream or Dream Whip.

Comment: A quick Sunday low calorie dessert! (Use chocolate pudding instead of pumpkin filling.)

Pumpkin Cream Cheese Pie

from Nadine Kruger, Campbell River, B.C.

Serves 8
Temperature is 300°
Baking time is 60 minutes

Ingredients:
Graham wafer pie shell
1 cup pumpkin
2 eggs
1/3 - 1/2 cup brown sugar
1 1/2 cups cream cheese
1 Tsp. cinnamon
1 Tsp. ginger
1/4 Tsp. nutmeg
1/4 Tsp. cloves
1 1/2 oz. orange juice

Method:
Combine all the ingredients in a
bowl with a blender. Pour mixture
into a pie shell. Bake for one hour.
Allow pie to cool then top with
whipping cream and pecans.

Notes

Chicken dishes

Chicken Jambalaya

from Lorna Penner, Kyuquot, B.C.

Temperature is 375°
Baking time is 1 1/2 hours
Uses a large roasting pan

Ingredients:

1 cut up chicken (good
    size)
2 cups chopped onions
1 cup chopped celery
3 cups uncooked rice
3 cups chicken stock
3 cups water
1/2 cup margarine
3 Tbsp. chopped parsley
2 pkgs. onion soup mix
salt and pepper
flour to coat chicken

Method:

Melt margarine.Brown chicken.
Remove. Add onions and celery.
Cook till half done. Add stock and
water and bring to boil. To this add
onion soup mix. Put rice in large
roasting pan. Add liquid and onions. Top with chicken. May save
some onion to put on top of chicken.
Cover. Bake till cooking well and
turn heat down to 300°. Serve with
lettuce salad.

Honey-Baked Chicken

from Merle Hagerty, Gold River, B.C.

Serves 6
Temperature is 350°
Baking time is 1 1/2 - 1 3/4 hours
Uses a shallow baking pan

Ingredients:

1 - 3 lb. fryer, cut up or
3 whole chicken breasts
1/3 cup melted margarine
1/3 cup honey
2 Tbsp. prepared mustard
1 Tsp. salt
1 Tsp. curry powder

Method:

Arrange chicken in shallow baking
pan, skin-side up. Combine the rest
of the ingredients and pour over the
chicken. Baste every 15 minutes.
Good served with rice.

Sharon's Herb-Breadcrumb Stuffing

from Esperanza Kitchen

Makes 1 1/2 cups

Ingredients:
- 1/4 cup butter
- 1/3 cup celery, chopped
- 1/3 cup onion, chopped
- 1 Tbsp. mayonnaise
- 1/2 Tsp. salt
- 1/4 Tsp. tarragon
- 1/8 Tsp. pepper
- 1 cup soft breadcrumbs

Method:
Saute celery and onions. Combine mayonnaise and splices. Mix in vegetables. Toss in breadcrumbs.

Chicken a la King

from Esperanza Kitchen

Serves 6

Ingredients:
- 1/2 cup margarine
- 2 Tbsp. onion
- 1 green pepper
- 1/2 lb. mushrooms
- 6 Tbsp. flour
- 1 cup chicken broth
- 1/2 Tsp. celery salt
- 1/8 Tsp. nutmeg
- 1/4 Tsp. pepper
- 1 cup milk
- 2 cups diced chicken
- 1/3 cup slivered pimento
- 1/2 cup ripe olives

Method:
Saute in 2 Tbsp. margarine, onion, green pepper, mushrooms. Melt remainder of 1/2 cup margarine in upper part of double boiler. Add flour. Stir until bubbly. Add gradually chicken broth. Cook over direct heat for 5 minutes. Add seasonings, milk, chicken, pimento and olives. Heat thoroughly over boiling water. Serve over rice or biscuits.

Captain's Chicken

from Colleen Shonwise, Tahsis, B.C.

Temperature is 350°
Baking time is 40 - 45 minutes

Ingredients:

1 cut up fryer, floured
1/4 cup butter
1/4 cup diced onions
1/2 cup diced green
  pepper
1 minced garlic clove
1 1/2 - 3 Tsp. curry pow-
  der
1/2 Tsp. thyme
2 cups canned tomatoes
3 Tbsp. raisins/currants
slivered almonds

Method:

Fry floured and cut up chicken. Remove from fry pan and put into casserole dish. Combine remaining ingredients and pour over chicken. Bake uncovered about 40 minutes or until chicken is tender. Sprinkle over top 3 Tbsp. raisins or currants and slivered almonds. Bake another 5 minutes. Serve over rice.

Chicken Rice Casserole

from Pearl Cochrane, Comox, B.C.

Temperature is 350°
Baking time is 60 minutes or till done
Uses an oblong pan

Ingredients:

1 cup white rice (not
  Minute Rice)
1 can cream of mushroom
  soup
1 can water plus a little
  more
1 pkge. dry onion soup
  mix
Small can mushrooms/
  liquid (optional)
Chicken pieces

Method:

Combine first five ingredients in pan and lay pieces of chicken on top. Bake.

Orange Curried Chicken

from Diane Bradford, Tofino, B.C.

Temperature is 350°
Baking time is 60 minutes
Uses a Casserole dish

Ingredients:
1 chicken cut up
Marinade ingredients:
1/4 cup melted butter or margarine
6 oz. can frozen orange juice
1/4 cup soya sauce
2 Tsp. curry powder
2 Tsp. ginger
1 Tsp. mustard powder

Method:
Combine marinade ingredients and pour over chicken. Marinate chicken for one hour then bake in open casserole dish. Serve with rice.

Lemon Chicken

from Angela McKenzie, Ucluelet, B.C.

Ingredients:
1 lb. chicken meat
3/4 Tsp. salt
1/2 Tsp. MSG
1 egg yolk
1/2 lemon
1 Tbsp. Worcestershire sauce
1 Tbsp. Ketchup
1 Tbsp. white vinegar
1 Tbsp. sugar
6 cups oil
1 Tbsp. cornstarch
7 Tbsp. water or lemon juice

Method:
Slice chicken into small pieces. Add 1/4 Tsp. salt, 1/4 Tsp. MSG, egg yolk. Mix well. Dredge in cornstarch. Slice lemon add Worcestershire sauce, Ketchup, vinegar, sugar, 1/2 Tsp. salt, MSG, water or lemon juice. Heat oil. Add chicken. Deep fry till golden. Remove. Drain. Boil lemon juice add 1/2 Tbsp. cornstarch and 1 Tbsp. oil to lemon juice. Pour over chicken and serve. Garnish with sliced tomato and cucumber.

Sweet & Sour Chicken

from Isabel McPherson, Whitby, Ont.

Ingredients:
- 1 cut up chicken
- 1/2 cup flour
- 1/2 cup white vinegar
- 1/2 cup brown sugar
- 1 1/2 Tsp. salt
- 1/4 Tsp. ginger
- 1/8 Tsp. pepper
- 1 med. orange, sliced
- 1 med. lemon, wedges

Method:
Dredge chicken in flour. Brown in frying pan. Combine vinegar, sugar, salt, ginger and pepper and mix well. Pour over chicken. Add orange slices and lemon wedges. Reduce heat and simmer chicken for 30 minutes or till tender.

Chicken Casserole

from Elsie Lindholm, Camrose, Alberta

Temperature is 350°
Baking time is 75 minutes

Ingredients:
- 1 med. chicken cut up
- 1/3 cup brown sugar
- 1/2 cup vinegar
- 1 cup water
- 1/2 cup Ketchup
- 3/4 cup onion
- 1 Tbsp. dry mustard
- 1 Tbsp. Worcestershire sauce
- salt
- pepper

Method:
Combine sugar, vinegar, water, Ketchup, onion, dry mustard, Worcestershire sauce, salt and pepper and pour over chicken. Bake in covered casserole 45 minutes at 350° then uncover and bake 30 - 40 minutes at 350° or more if needed. Rice and peas go well with this casserole.

Chicken Pot Pie

from JoAnne Lightbody, New Market, Ont.

Temperature is 400°
Baking time is Until pastry is done
Uses a 9 x 13 inch baking dish

Ingredients:

1 1/2 cups diced carrots
2 cups diced celery
2 cups diced potatoes
1 small sliced onion
3 cups diced cooked
  chicken or turkey
1 can cream of chicken
  soup
1/3 cup flour
1/2 Tsp. salt
1/4 Tsp. pepper
Pastry for top
2 slices bacon

Method:

Cook in saucepan - carrots, celery, potatoes, onion with 2 slices of bacon (for flavour) until just tender. Drain, remove bacon. Combine with chicken. Combine chicken soup, flour, salt, pepper and heat till bubbles. Add 2 cups chicken stock and stir to blend until it thickens. Pour over chicken and vegetables. Put in casserole. Cover with slashed pastry.

Grandma's Chicken Stew

from Hanne Reid, Steinbech, Manitoba

Temperature is 350°
Baking time is 1 1/2 hours
Uses a 9 x 13 inch pan

Ingredients:

3 - 4 lb chicken pieces
1/2 cup Ketchup
1/4 cup soya sauce
1/2 Tsp. onion powder
1/2 Tsp. MSG (optional)
1/4 Tsp. garlic powder
1 sliced onion
1 sliced tomato

Method:

Wash chicken, dry. Mix Ketchup, soya sauce and all of the seasonings in a large bowl. Put chicken pieces in and coat well. Place in baking dish. Add tomatoes and onions. Add a little water, scrape bowl and pour over chicken. Cover with tin foil. Bake till tender. Serve over rice.

Hungarian Chicken Paprikish

from Mames McPherson, Toronto, Ont.

Ingredients:
- oil
- celery
- green pepper
- tomato
- onion
- 3 Tsp. paprika
- chicken
- water

Method:
Brown onion in oil. Add celery, green pepper, tomato. Add paprika. Brown chicken. Add a little water at a time. Simmer 1 1/2 hours. Goes well with rice or macaroni. Nice with sour cream or yogurt.

Baked Chicken Salad

from Betsy Patton, Bellingham, Wash.

Serves 6
Temperature is 350D
Baking time is 25 minutes
Uses a Buttered large casserole dish

Ingredients:
- 6 cups cooked, cut up chicken
- 4 cups celery
- 1 cup salted, sliced almonds
- 4 Tbsp. chopped, green pepper
- 2 Tbsp. grated onion
- 4 Tbsp. pimento
- 3 Tbsp. fresh lemon juice
- 1 Tsp. salt
- 1 1/2 cups mayonnaise
- 1 1/2 cups grated American cheese
- 2 cups Chinese noodles

Method:
Combine all except cheese and Chinese noodles. Mix well and put in buttered casserole. Sprinkle cheese and noodles on top. Bake - do not overbake. Serve hot.

Teriyaki Marinade

from Sandy Barnett, Ucluelet, B.C.

Makes For 2 lbs. fish

Ingredients:
- 1/2 cup cooking oil
- 1/4 cup soy sauce
- 1/2 cup vinegar
- 1 Tbsp. grated fresh gingeroot or
- 1 Tsp. ground ginger
- 1 clove garlic
- 2 Tbsp. molasses.

Method:

Combine oil, soy sauce, vinegar, ginger and garlic. Place chicken, beef or pork in plastic bag set in deep bowl or shallow baking dish. Pour marinade mixture over meat. Close bag or cover dish. Refrigerate 4 - 6 hours or overnight. Turn bag or spoon marinade over meat occasionally to coat evenly. Drain - reserve marinade. Stir in molasses. Baste meat last ten minutes of barbecuing.

Notes

West Coast Specialties

Impossible Tuna Quiche

from Gloria Pottage, Victoria, B.C.

Temperature is 400°
Baking time is 30 - 40 minutes
Uses two 8 inch or one 10 inch pie plate, buttered

Ingredients:
FILLING:
  1 can tuna
  1 med. onion chopped
  1 stalk celery chopped
TOPPING:
  2 cups milk
  4 eggs
  1/2 cup flour
  1/2 Tsp. each salt/pepper
  grated cheese

Method:
Put fillings into pan (preferably glass). Blend milk, eggs, flour, seasonings and pour on top. Sprinkle on cheese.

Comment:
Another suggestion for the filling would be: salmon, ham, broccoli, peas, carrots or combination.

Fish Noodle Casserole

from Esperanza Kitchen

Temperature is 350°
Uses a 1 1/2 Quart Casserole, buttered

Ingredients:
  1 - 12 oz. pkg. noodles
  2 - 71/2 oz. cans drained
    fish
  2 - 10 oz. cans of soup
    (mushroom,etc)
or 1 - 10 oz. can cheddar
    cheese soup and 1 cup
    milk

Method:
Put into boiling water the noodles. Cook till tender. Drain. Add the soup of your choice. Stir. Bake.

Tuna Macaroni Casserole

from Bernice Bolton, Gold River, B.C.

Temperature is 350°
Baking time is 30 - 40 minutes
Uses a 2 Quart casserole dish, buttered

Ingredients:

1 - 7 oz. can tuna
1 can cream of mushroom
soup
1 cup chopped onion
2 Tsp. butter
3/4 cup milk
1 cup celery
4 cups cooked macaroni
salt/pepper
1 Tsp. soya sauce

Method:

Cook macaroni and drain. Saute celery, onions in butter. Combine all ingredients. Bake.

Salmon Casserole

from Esperanza Kitchen

Temperature is 325°
Baking time is 20 minutes
Uses a 1 1/2 quart casserole dish, buttered

Ingredients:

1 can mushroom soup (10 oz.)
1/2 cup milk
1 cup cubed process cheese
2 cups noodles
1 (7 3/4 oz.) can salmon, flaked
1/2 cup Chinese noodles

Method:

Heat in top of double boiler mushroom soup and milk. When smoothly blended and hot add process cheese. Heat until cheese melts. Combine noodles and salmon. Add cheese sauce and sprinkle Chinese noodles on top. Bake.

Mrs. McLean's Salmon Rolls

from Lois Hooks, Edmonton, Alta.

Temperature is 425°
Baking time is 20 - 30 minutes

Ingredients:

1 recipe of biscuit dough
on page 12
1 pint of canned salmon
1 can of mushroom soup
Dash of lemon juice
Salt/pepper

Method:

Roll out biscuit dough as for cinnamon buns. Spread with butter. Mix salmon, soup, lemon juice, salt, pepper well. Spread generously over biscuit dough. Roll up. Slice about 1 inch thick and place on cookie sheet. Bake. Serve with white cream sauce.

West Coast Salmon Quiche

from Lucille Collins, Tahsis, B.C.

Temperature is 350°
Baking time is 30 - 35 minutes
9 x 13 inch baking pan or quiche pan

Ingredients:

CRUST:
3 cups all purpose flour
1 Tsp. salt
2/3 cup vegetable oil
1/4 cup plus 2 Tbsp. milk
FILLING:
1 cup Monteray Jack
Cheese, shredded
1 - 1 1/2 cups flaked
cooked salmon
5 eggs
2 cups half & half (cream)
3/4 Tsp. salt
1/8 Tsp. pepper
dash ground nutmeg
2 Tbsp. snipped fresh
parsley

Method:

In medium bowl mix flour, salt, oil and milk lightly with fork until blended. Pat in pan about 1 inch thick, up sides of pan. Bake 8 min. Put cheese over hot crust then the fish. In small mixing bowl blend eggs, milk, salt, pepper and nutmeg. Pour over fish. Sprinkle with parsley. Bake until knife inserted in centre comes out clean about 30 - 35 min. Cool for 10 minutes. Serve with green salad.

Comment: "I sometimes use duck eggs."

Impossible Salmon Broccoli Pie

from Ruby Quiring, Regina, Saskatchewan

Temperature is 400°
Baking time is 30 - 40 minutes
Uses a pie plate, buttered

Ingredients:
- 1 1/2 cups chopped frozen/fresh broccoli
- 3 cups grated cheddar cheese
- 1 - 7 oz. can salmon
- 2/3 cup chopped onion
- 1 1/3 cups milk
- 3 eggs
- 3/4 cup Bisquick mix (pg.11)
- 3/4 Tsp. salt
- 1/4 Tsp. pepper

Method:
Rinse broccoli under running cold water to thaw; drain. Mix broccoli, 2 cups of the cheese, the salmon and onion in plate. Beat milk, eggs, Bisquick Mix, salt and pepper until smooth. Pour into plate. Bake until knife inserted in centre comes out clean. Top with remaining cheese. Bake until cheese is melted, one or two minutes longer. Cool five minutes.

Comment:
1 1/2 cups cooked, cut-up chicken can be used in place of salmon.

Salmon Croquettes

from Audrey Dol, Tahsis, B.C.

Ingredients:
- 1 lb. salmon
- 1 cup milk
- 4 Tbsp. butter
- 1 Tbsp. lemon juice
- 1/2 cup flour
- 1/2 Tsp. salt
- 1 cup fine, dry bread crumbs
- 1 egg, optional
- fat or oil

Method:
Melt the butter and stir in flour. Cook for a moment to cook starch in the flour. Add the milk and heat over medium heat until smooth and thick. Add the salt and lemon juice. Bone the salmon, flake it and add to the cream sauce. Set aside and allow to cool. When mixture is firm, shape it into small cakes or balls. Dip in flour and beaten egg then the bread crumbs. Fry till brown turning once.

Salmon in a Crust

from Colleen Shonwise, Tahsis, B.C.

Temperature is 375°
Baking time is 60 minutes or till golden

Ingredients:

Pastry for two crusts
1 clove minced garlic
1/4 cup melted butter (divided)
2 medium onions, chopped
1/2 cup Parmesan cheese
1/2 cup fresh bread-crumbs
3 hard boiled eggs, chopped
1 pint salmon, drained
1/3 cup fresh chopped dill or 1 Tbsp. dry dill
1 cup sour cream
1 egg yolk
1/4 Tsp. salt

Method:

Prepare pastry. Saute onion and garlic in 2 Tbsp. butter. Combine crumbs and cheese. Divide pastry in 2 (1 part larger). Roll out to 7x9. Put on cooking sheet with 1 inch border. Sprinkle with layers of half crumb mixture, half onion, salmon, eggs, dill then remaining crumb mixture and onions. Drizzle butter on top. Spread with sour cream. Combine egg yolk, salt. Brush borders with mixture. Roll out 2nd pastry to 10x12. Place over ingredients, seal, flute. Decorate and bake.

Comments:

Decorate top with remaining dough into a salmon shape. Slice small openings in top to allow steam to escape. Let dish sit for 10 minutes before cutting. Unusual dish which tastes extraordinary.

Smoked Salmon Paté

from Eleanor Snyder, Edmonton, Alta.

Ingredients:

3 1/2 oz. smoked salmon
4 hard boiled eggs
1/2 cup butter
1 Tbsp. dill weed
1 Tbsp. lemon juice
salt
pepper

Method:

Blend salmon and eggs. Add butter, dill and lemon juice. Mix till smooth and season with salt and pepper to taste. Serve at room temperature. Great on crackers.

Salmon Loaf

from Lillian Parry

Temperature is 350°
Baking time is 45 minutes
Uses a Loaf pan

Ingredients:
- 3 cups salmon - shredded
- 2 1/2 cups scalded milk
- 2 cups dried bread crumbs or crackers
- 1 Tbsp. lemon juice or vinegar
- salt/pepper/accent
- 1 Tbsp. grated onion
- 3 eggs yolks
- 3 egg whites

Method:
Put bread or cracker crumbs in hot milk. Add to salmon, vinegar, spices, onion and yolks. Mix well. Beat egg whites separately. Fold in last. Bake.

Note: A similar recipe was also submitted by Alma Cunningham of Victoria.

Crab Fettuccine

from Diane Bradford, Tofino, B.C.

Ingredients:
- 1/2 cup butter
- 1 or 2 cloves of garlic, crushed
- 1 can or 1/2 lb. fresh crab
- 3/4 cup whipping cream
- salt/pepper
- 1/2 cup Parmesan cheese approx.
- 12 oz.cooked,fresh Fettuccine pasta

Method:
Heat butter, garlic, crab, whipping cream, salt, pepper and cheese together. Pour over cooked pasta.

Ginger and Onion Crab

from Angela McKenzie, Ucluelet, B.C.

Ingredients:
- cooked crab (any size)
- ginger (few pieces)
- green onion (3 or 4 few pieces)
- garlic (3 or 4 few pieces)
- 1/4 Tsp. salt
- 1/2 Tsp. soy sauce
- 1 Tbsp. Sesame oil
- 1 Tbsp. cornstarach
- 1/4 Tbsp. sugar

Method:
Remove shell from crab. Wash and cut into smaller pieces. Break the leg with back of knife. Combined seasoning: Mix salt, soy sauce, sesame oil, cornstarch and sugar. Heat oil in pan. Add garlic, ginger and green onions. Stir fry over high heat for 10 to 15 minutes. Add combined seasonings and crab. Simmer and remove to a plate. Garnish with parsley and serve.

Nootka Island Clam Pie

from Mark Vance, Anacortes, Wash.

Temperature is 350°
Baking time is 1 hour - watch
Uses a 9 inch pie plate

Ingredients:
- 1 pint clams, chopped fine
- 1 egg, well beaten
- 4 soda crackers, finely crushed
- 1/2 cup clam nectar
- butter
- salt and pepper
- 1/2 cup milk
- 1 small onion, chopped
- Prepare favourite rich pastry

Method:
Line pie plate with pastry. Put in a layer of clams, sauted onions and crumbs. Beat egg, add clam nectar and milk and pour over clams. Cover with pastry. Bake.

Fried Shrimp
with Garlic Dressing

from Angela McKenzie, Ucluelet, B.C.

Ingredients:

1 1/4 lb. large shrimps
1 Tsp. salt
1/2 red pepper
1/4 Tsp. black pepper
3 green onions
6 cups oil
5 garlic cloves
2 Tbsp. apple cider
1 Tsp. MSG
Radishs, cherry tomatoes,
cucumbers, parsley

Method:

Clean shrimps with salted water and drain. Dry. Shred red pepper, green onions and garlic. Heat oil in pan and put shrimps in it. Deep fry for one minute and remove. Stir-fry the shreds of pepper, green onion and garlic with 2 tablespoons of oil. Add cider, salt, pepper. Stir-fry again. Remove immediately. Garnish with vegetables.

Long Beach Crab Quiche

from Esperanza Kitchen

Uses a Pie plate

Ingredients:

4 eggs
1/2 cup onion
1/4 cup green pepper
1 Tsp. celery salt
2 cups light cream
1/8 Tsp. cayenne red
   pepper
Meat from 2 or 3 crab or
2 - 7 1/2 oz. tin crab,
   drained
1 cup white cheese
Snipped parsley
Pastry

Method:

Line a nine inch pie plate with pastry. Lightly saute onion and green pepper in margarine or butter. In a separate dish beat eggs until blended. Add onion and pepper. Add cream, celery, salt and pepper. Sprinkle crabmeat and shredded cheese into pastry. Sprinkle with a few dashes of lemon juice. Pour egg mixture over all. Sprinkle with parsley. Bake at 350° for 40 - 45 minutes.

Comment:

You can use Swiss or mozzarella or plain Philadelphia cheese.

Seafood Souffle

from Esperanza Kitchen

Temperature is 375°
Baking time is 30 min. till puffed and browned
Uses a 2 Quart casserole dish, buttered

Ingredients:

1 cup clams (shrimp/
  prawns) chopped
liquid of seafood
1/2 - 3/4 cup milk
4 Tbsp. butter or marga-
  rine
1/4 cup finely chopped
  onions
5 Tbsp. flour
5 egg yolks
1/2 Tsp. salt
1/2 Tsp. celery salt
6 egg whites
1 1/2 cups corn, frozen or
  fresh

Method:

Measure liquid, add enough milk to make 1 cup. Heat till bubbly. Melt 3 Tbsp. of margarine in pan. and cook onions till soft. Remove. Add 4 Tbsp. flour. Stir till smooth. Add liquids. Beat vigourously with whisk. Return to stove. Cook till smooth and thick. Remove. Beat egg yolks into mixture 1 at a time. In a separate bowl beat egg whites till stiff formed peaks. Stir 3 Tbsp. whites into liquid mix. Mix corn with flour. Stir corn and shell fish into sauce. Fold in 3 egg whites. Bake.

Oyster Stew

from Esperanza Kitchen

Ingredients:

2 dozen shucked oysters
1/2 cup butter or marga-
  rine
1 Tbsp. Worcestershire
  sauce
1 Tsp. celery salt
1 quart of milk
Dash of pepper

Method:

Melt butter in kettle. Add chopped oysters along with the liquid. Heat until the edges of oysters curl slightly. Add milk and seasonings. Do not boil. Add a dash of paprika and a spot of butter into hot bowls of stew.

Mussel-Rice Salad
with curried dressing

from Isabel McPherson, Whitby, Ont.

Ingredients:
- 1 1/2 cups long grain rice
- 2 Tbsp. oil
- 3 lb. mussels
- 3 cloves garlic, minced
- 1 onion finely chopped
- 1 cup dry white wine
- 1/4 cup chopped fresh parsley
- 1 bunch water cress

Method:
Cook rice, drain with cold water. Toss with oil. Cook onion and garlic in butter till tender. Stir in mussels, wine, parsley. Cook covered for 5 minutes till mussels open. Let cool in liquid. Remove mussels from shells, pat dry. Stir into rice. Boil mussel cooking liquid to 1/4 cup. Let cool. Pour over mussels and rice. Toss with dressing.

Mussel & Rice Salad Dressing

from Isabel McPherson, Whitby, Ont.

Serves 6 - 8

Ingredients:
- egg
- lemon juice
- curry powder
- mustard
- salt
- oil

Method:
In blender, blend egg, lemon juice, curry powder, mustard and salt. With motor running gradually add oil in a thin and steady stream. (If not consistency of mayonnaise, blend one egg for 20 seconds and slowly add thin sauce with motor running.) Pour dressing over mussels and rice, toss, transfer to salad bowl. Surround with water cress leaves.

Kebabs on the Rocks

from Mark Vance, Anacortes, Wash.

Temperature is 475°

Ingredients:

48 mussels (2 - 3 lbs.)
1 1/4 cups cider
Mixed herbs (basil, fennel, thyme)
1 small onion
5 peppercorns
1 bay leaf
1 garlic clove
4 sprigs of parsley
4 slices of bacon
1 Tbsp. melted butter
SAUCE
2 Tbsp. olive oil
1 chopped onion
1 1/2 lb. tomatoes peeled and chopped
1 Tsp. salt
1/2 Tsp. pepper/oregano
2 sage leaves
4 drops Tabasco
1/2 cup cider

Method:

Wash and brush mussels thoroughly. Bring cider to boil with herbs, onion, peppercorns, bay leaf, garlic and parsley. Add mussels. Cover. Cook 10 - 15 minutes until shells open. Stir frequently. Remove mussels from shells. Thread 12 mussels on each skewer. Roll a slice of bacon around the length of skewer. Baste with butter. Place on baking sheet. Broil in very hot oven 4 inches from heat until bacon is brown and crisp.

SAUCE:

Heat oil in skillet. Add onion and garlic. Add tomatoes, simmer gently with lid on for 10 minutes. Add spices. Pour in cider. Simmer additional 10 minutes. When cider has evaporated, sieve the sauce, pour back into pan. Check seasonings. Cover over low heat. The longer the sauce cooks the better.

Camp Fire
Oysters, Clams, Mussels.

from Esperanza Kitchen

Ingredients:

Oysters/clams/mussels
melted butter
lemon juice

Method:

Scrub shell fish well. Place on grill over an open fire. Roast for about 15 minutes till shells open. Eat dipping into melted butter with lemon juice.

Clam Sauce

from Judy Ellis, Tahsis, B.C.

Makes 1 portion

Ingredients:
- 1 Tbsp. sour cream
- 1 Tbsp. garlic butter
- 1/2 Tsp. lemon juice
- 1 dash cayenne pepper
- clams

Method:
Mix all ingredients together and cook over low heat for 10 minutes - approximately or till clams have cooked. Be careful to use low temperature so sour cream doesn't separate.

Comment:
This recipe is for one portion only so for ten people multiply by 10

Quick Shrimp & Clam Sauce

from Cindi Vance, Anacortes, Wash.

Ingredients:
- 6 Tbsp. olive oil
- 3 minced cloves garlic
- 3/4 cup finely chopped parsley
- 1 cup minced clams with liquid
- 1/2 lb. shelled raw shrimp pieces
- 1/8 Tsp. oregano
- pepper

Method:
Heat oil in skillet. Add garlic and cook gently for 5 minutes. Add remaining ingredients. Heat until bubbly and shrimp is pink. Serve over hot cooked sea shell pasta or spaghetti pasta. Top with grated Paresan or Romano cheese.

Comment:
If you like more liquid add 4 oz. clam juice. Also may use part butter and part olive oil for richer flavour.

Stuffed Baked Fish

from Esperanza Kitchen

Temperature is 425°
Baking time is 45 minutes

Ingredients:

1 med. salmon, coho or
   spring
4 cups finely crumbled
   bread
1/2 cup melted margarine
   or drippings
1 diced medium onion
1/2 Tsp. salt
dash of pepper
1 1/2 Tsp. sage
1/4 Tsp. celery salt
1 Tbsp. parsley
1 egg
dash of paprika

Method:

Clean fish and combine remaining ingredients. Pack into fish. Optional - put a few slices of bacon on top of fish and cover with tomato juice, baste occasionally. Brush top of fish with margarine. Bake.

Easy Fish Bake

from Esperanza Kitchen

Temperature is 350°
Baking time is 12 - 15 minutes
Uses a 9 inch square pan

Ingredients:

1 lb. fish (cod, snapper)
1/4 cup margarine
1 small onion, chopped
salt
1/4 Tsp. minced parsley
1/4 cup dried bread-
   crumbs (optional)

Method:

Saute onion in margarine. Pour onion into pan. Dip fish fillets in onion/margarine mixture, coating both sides. Arrange in pan in single layer. Sprinkle fish with salt, parsley and dried bread-crumbs. Bake until fish flakes easily when tested with fork.

Clam Souffle

from Nancy Symington, Tofino, B.C.

Serves 6
Temperature is 350°
Baking time is 40 - 45 minutes till puffy/golden
Uses a 2 Quart casserole dish, buttered

Ingredients:
1 cup milk
1 1/2 cups crumbled soda
   crackers
1/4 cup melted margarine
1 can (8 oz.) clams,
   drained, rinsed
1 chopped green pepper
1 chopped onion
salt & pepper
dash of Worcestershire
   sauce
2 eggs, well beaten

Method:
Combine milk and crackers in a bowl and let soak for 5 minutes. Add margarine, clams, green pepper, onions, salt, pepper, worcestershire sauce and eggs. Mix well. Pour into casserole dish and bake. Serve at once.

Baked Cod Fillets

from Esperanza Kitchen

Makes 6 servings
Temperature is 450°

Ingredients:
2 lb. fish, cod or halibut
3/4 cup bread-crumbs
1 Tbsp. vinegar
1 Tbsp. Worcestershire
   sauce
1 Tbsp. lemon juice
1/2 cup melted butter
1 Tsp. prepared mustard
1 Tsp. salt
1/8 Tsp. pepper

Method:
Sprinkle bottom of greased baking dish with bread-crumbs. Wipe fish with damp cloth and place over bread-crumbs. Mix remaining ingredients and pour over fish. Sprinkle with paprika and baste several times. Bake.

Comment:
Fresh fish - 10 min. per inch thickness. Frozen fish - 20 min. per inch thickness. Red Snapper is a favourite fish.

Baked Salmon Steaks

from Colleen Shonwise, Tahsis, B.C.

Serves 6
Temperature is 400°
Baking time is 15 minutes or until steaks flake

Ingredients:
- 6 salmon steaks
- salt
- pepper
- 2 Tbsp. butter or margarine
- 1/2 cup chopped celery
- 1/4 cup chopped onions
- 3/4 cup fine bread crumbs
- 1/4 cup Ketchup
- 1/2 Tsp. Worcestershire sauce

Method:
Season salmon with salt and pepper. In heated fry pan add butter and onions. Cook onions and celery until transparent then add bread crumbs, Worcestershire sauce and Ketchup. Place salmon steaks on greased cooking sheets, sprinkle crumb mixture over steaks and bake.

Salmon Sauce

from Laura Brisbane, Bellingham, Wash.

Temperature is 300°
Baking time is 25 minutes

Ingredients:
- 1/2 lb. of melted butter
- 1/4 cup Ketchup
- 4 Tbsp. soy sauce
- 2 Tbsp. mustard
- 1/8 - 1/4 cup brown sugar
- Dash of Worcestershire sauce
- 1 clove garlic or garlic powder

Method:
Butter fry salmon. Baste before, during and after cooking. Bake.

#1 Bar-b-que Marinade for Salmon

from Esperanza Kitchen

Uses a shallow pan

Ingredients:
- 1/2 cup Ketchup
- 1/4 cup salad oil
- 3 Tbsp. lemon juice
- 2 Tbsp. vinegar
- 1 Tsp. Worcestershire sauce
- 1 Tsp. salt
- 1/2 Tsp. grated onion
- 1/2 Tsp. dry mustard
- 1/4 Tsp. paprika
- 1 clove garlic, chopped
- 3 drops of Tabasco sauce

Method:
Combine ingredients. Pour over fish in shallow pan and let stand in fridge for at least 30 minutes. Cook about 4 inches over hot coals for about 8 - 10 minutes on each side.

#2 Bar-b-que Marinade for Salmon

from Esperanza Kitchen

For 2 lbs. of fish
Uses a shallow pan

Ingredients:
- 3 Tbsp. lemon juice
- 1 Tsp. grated lemon rind
- 1/4 cup salad oil
- 1/2 Tsp. salt
- 1/8 Tsp. pepper
- 1/4 Tsp. marjoram
- 1 Tbsp. finely chopped onion

Method:
Combine ingredients and pour over fish in pan. Let stand in fridge for at least 30 minutes. Cook about 4 inches over hot coals - 8 to 10 minutes on each side.

Keta (fish) in Court

from Marilyn Atleo, Vancouver, B.C.

Uses a shallow poaching pan

Ingredients:

2 lbs. centre cut salmon (keta) or white fish fillets
1 small whole onion coarsley chopped
1 medium carrot coarsley chopped
2 cups water
1 Tsp. salt
1/3 cup lemon juice or wine vinegar
1 cube vegetable bouillon
2 bay leaves
2 stalks of celery with leaves
2 Tbsp. cold water
1 Tbsp. cornstarch

Method:

Add vegetables, water, salt, lemon juice and bouillon to saucepan. Bring to boil, cover, simmer liquid 20 - 30 min. Place fish pieces skin side down in pan. Strain liquid over fish. Cover. Slowly bring liquid to boil, simmer about 10 min. Test for doneness. Then remove it to warming platter. Reduce liquid in pan to 1 cup, thicken with cornstarch in cold water. Simmer until slightly thickened. Pour sauce over fish or serve on side.

Lemon Rice Stuffing for Salmon

from Sandy Barnett, Ucluelet, B.C.

Temperature is 400°

Ingredients:

1/3 cup melted margarine
1 cup chopped celery
1/3 cup chopped onion
3 cups cooked rice
1/2 Tsp. salt
1/2 Tsp. Thyme
1 Tbsp. lemon juice
Grated rind of one lemon

Method:

Saute celery and onion in margarine. Combine all ingredients and stuff salmon or any fish. Bake fish 15 minutes for each inch of thickness of fish.

Chinese Stir-Fry Fish

from Esperanza Kitchen

Ingredients:

1 - 2 lb. fish, cod or halibut
cornstarch
2 - 3 Tbsp. oil
3 cups thinly sliced
  vegetables*
1 Tbsp. oil
1 clove garlic, minced
2 minced green onions
2 slices fresh ginger root,
  minced (optional)
or 1/2 Tsp. ground ginger
1 cup broth or stock or
  water
2 Tbsp. soya sauce
3 Tbsp. vinegar
3 Tbsp. brown sugar
1/2 Tsp. salt
2 Tsp. cornstarch

Method:

Cut fish in bite-size pieces against grain. Dredge in cornstarch. Brown quickly in oil. *While fish browns prepare vegetables (cabbage, carrots, celery, onions or mushrooms, etc.) Remove fish from pan. Stir-fry minced garlic, green onions and ginger root for one minute. Add vegetables. Stir- fry one minute. Add remaining ingredients and bring to boil. Return fish to pan. Simmer, covered for five minutes. Serve over rice.

Process for Smoked Fish

from Esperanza Kitchen

Ingredients:

1 Tsp. celery salt
1 Tsp. onion salt
1 Tsp. garlic salt
1/2 cup pickling salt
2 cups brown sugar

Method:

Layer fish in large pan. Sprinkle each layer with the above ingredients. Leave over night. Drain, rinse gently with fresh water. Wipe with paper towel. Place on rack in smoke house.

Pickled Salmon

from Myrna Hill, M.V. Anastasis - YWAM

Uses a crock pot or plastic pail

Ingredients:
- salmon
- rock salt
- vinegar (3 parts to 1 part water)
- onion slices
- pickling spice (1 Tbsp. per layer)

Method:
Fillet fresh salmon into 4x6 inch wedges. Cover bottom of crock with rock salt, layer fish/salt/fish/salt till all fillets are covered. Place plate on top. Let sit 10 days. Water will form in 24 hrs. To freshen fish, rinse 3 times in fresh water at 8 hr. intervals between rinses. Fill jars alternating layers of onions/fish/pickling spice. When jar is filled, fill with vinegar & water. Let sit 6 weeks. Serve with crackers & sour cream or as plain pickles.

Note: When layering do not let fish touch sides or other fillets.

Sea Cucumber Puffs

from Mark Vance, Anacortes, Wash.

Ingredients:
- 1 Tbsp. melted butter
- 1 egg
- 1 cup milk
- 1/2 Tsp. salt
- 1 Tbsp. baking powder
- 1 1/2 cups flour
- 1 Pt. fresh sea cucumber meat or clams
- oil

Method:
Beat egg and add butter and milk. Sift baking powder and salt with the flour. Add to egg and milk mixture. Squeeze out any excess water from the sea cucumber meat. Grind or finely chop the meat and mix with butter. Make in balls size of walnut. Deep fat fry. Clams may be substituted for sea cucumber.

Salmon on the Beach

from Esperanza Kitchen

Ingredients:
Pacific Coho or Spring
salmon
melted margarine
chopped onions
lemon juice

Method:
Prepare fish for supper on the beach. Generously sprinkle lemon juice on inside. Fill cavity with onions. Place fish on two layers of tin foil, shiny side out, edges turned up. Pour mixture of lemon juice and margarine over fish. Sprinkle with salt. Fold tin foil carefully around fish, 1 sheet at a time carefully avoiding making holes. Make a hot fire on beach removing all burning fire logs when ready. Place fish in hot sands or rock. Cover with hot sand or rocks. Bake about one hour.

Clams on the Beach

from Esperanza Kitchen

Cooking time is 30 - 45 minutes

Ingredients:
seaweed
clams
butter
lemon juice

Method:
Dig a fair size pit on a sandy or rocky beach. Build a nice active fire in the pit. While it burns for an hour or so dig clams if there is not a warning for red tide. Gather seaweed. When the sand or rocks have become very hot put some seaweed into pit. Then toss clams over seaweed and cover with more seaweed. Steamed in the seaweed and dipped in sun-melted butter combined with a generous squeeze of lemon juice.A taste experience you will never forget.

129

Uncle John's Cod Mulligan

from Helen Ottom, Campbell River, B.C.

Ingredients:
2 medium potatoes, cubed
1 medium onion, cut fine
1/2 cup white rice
salt/pepper
1 small tin tomatoes
1 lb. or less fresh cod
    fillets

Method:
Place all ingredients in a pot. Cover with water and simmer until rice and potatoes are done.

Fish Batter

from Eleanor Snyder, Edmonton, Alta.

Ingredients:
2/3 cup cornstarch
1/3 cup flour
1 Tsp. vinegar
3/4 cup water
1 Tbsp. baking powder

Method:
Mix cornstarch, flour, vinegar and water. Refrigerate until cold. Add one tablespoon of baking powder and mix. Dip fish (patted dry) into batter and deep fry until golden on each side.

Crispy Batter

from Esperanza Kitchen

Makes Enough for 2 lbs. fish

Ingredients:
1 cup flour
2 Tbsp. baking powder
1 1/2 Tsp. salt
2 Tsp. sugar
1 Tbsp. oil
1 cup water

Method:
Combine all ingredients. Makes sufficient amount for 2 pounds of fish. Deep fry.

Bread-Crumbs Stuffing for Fish

from Esperanza Kitchen

Ingredients:
- 1 cup grated carrot
- 2 medium onions chopped
- 1/4 cup butter or margarine
- 2 cups dry bread-crumbs
- 1 egg
- 2 Tsp. salt
- 1 cup fresh cut up mushrooms
- 1/2 cup snipped parsley
- 1 1/2 Tbsp. lemon juice
- 1 clove garlic minced
- 1/4 Tsp. marjoram
- 1/4 Tsp. pepper

Method:
Cook and stir onion in butter until tender. Lightly mix in remaining ingredients.

Fish Marinade

from Isabel McPherson, Whitby, Ont.

For 2 lbs. of fish

Ingredients:
- 1/4 cup vegetable oil
- 3 Tbsp. lemon juice
- 1 Tbsp. finely chopped onion
- 1/2 Tsp. dried mixed herbs*
- 1 Tbsp. finely chopped onion
- Pinch of pepper
- 1/2 Tsp. salt

Method:
Place fish in a single layer in shallow dish. Combine marinade ingredients and pour over fish. Marinate for 30 minutes turning once. Grill, bar-b-que or bake at 375° for approximately 15 minutes until fish flakes easily with a fork.

*You can us thyme, rosemary and basil for the dried herbs.

Pacific Northwest Clam Chowder

from Mark Vance, Anacotes, Wash.

Serves 4

Ingredients:
- 1 1/2 cups chopped clams
- 3 Tbsp. salt pork, minced
- 1 small onion
- 1 1/4 cups clam broth
- 2 cups diced potatoes
- 2 pints half and half cream
- salt & pepper
- 1 Tbsp. butter

Method:

Cook salt pork in soup pot over medium heat until cracklings are lightly browned. Add onion, pepper. Cook till onion is transparent but not browned. Add clam broth. Stir in potatoes. Simmer uncovered till potatoes become tender — about 10 to 14 minutes. Liquid will reduce slightly. Add cream. Heat thoroughly but do not boil. Add salt to taste. Simmer for 2 hours. Add clams. Heat through. Correct seasonings. You may add butter just before serving.

Comment:

Large clams are best suited to chowder and you can make an excellent and distinctively North West version by using geoduck. To prepare geoduck cut it from the shell. Dip the neck in hot water for 30 seconds. Then cut away the skin and entrails. Slice the meat diagonally into thin strips.

Tim's Batter

from Tim Bird, Esperanza, B.C.

Ingredients:
- 2/3 cup cornstarch
- 1/2 cup flour
- 1 Tbsp. butter
- water
- 1 Tbsp. vinegar

Method:

Mix dry ingredients with flour to a medium thickness. Chill for to 2 to 3 hours. The colder the better. Just before using, add vinegar. Deep fry immediatly.

Meat dishes

Mushroom Meatballs

from Marion McLean

Makes 4 servings

Ingredients:
- 1 can mushroom soup
- 1/2 cup water
- 1/4 cup of soup mixture
- 1 lb. ground beef
- 1/2 cup of fine dry bread crumbs
- 2 Tbsp. minced onion
- 1 Tbsp. minced parsley
- 1 egg, slightly beaten
- 1/4 Tsp. salt

Method:
Shape into meatballs about 1 1/2 inch diameter. Brown in 1 table-spoon shortening in large skillet. Add remaining soup mixture. Cover and cook over low heat about 15 minutes stirring occasionally.

Sweet & Sour Sauce for Meatballs

from Connie Heinrick, Richmond, B.C.

Makes Approx. 2 cups

Ingredients:
- 1 cup tomato sauce
- 1 cup water
- 1/4 cup vinegar
- 2 Tbsp. brown sugar
- 1 Tsp. salt
- 1 Tsp. celery seed
- 1 Tbsp. instant minced onion

Method:
Brown meatballs in shortening. Combine all ingredients. Put meatballs in sauce. Boil or bake until desired consistency.

Comment:
Serve on rice, noodles or spaghetti. Serve with lots of green vegetables.

Meatballs and Dumplings

from Audrey Barnett, Port Coquitlam, B.C

Feeds 4 hungry men

Ingredients:
1 lb. ground beef
leftover vegetables
1 - 19 oz. tin vegetable
   soup
1/2 tin water
Dumplings:
1 cup flour
1 Tsp. baking powder
1/2 Tsp. salt
1/2 cup milk
2 Tbsp. cooking oil

Method:
Make your favourite meatball recipe into 1 inch balls and brown. Put in covered casserole dish. Add leftover vegetables. Next add tin vegetable soup plus water. Put in 375° oven. Then make dumplings by combining flour, salt, oil, baking powder and milk. These should be stiff. Drop by spoonfuls on top of casserole. Bake for 30 minutes or till done. Do not uncover till done.

Sweet & Sour Meatballs

from Colleen Shonwise, Tahsis, B.C.

Ingredients:
1 lb. ground beef
1/4 cup dry crumbs
2 Tbsp. finely chopped
   onions
1/2 Tsp. salt
1/8 Tsp. pepper
1 Tbsp. shortening
1/4 cup sugar
1 - 14 oz. tin crushed
   pineapple
2 Tbsp. cornstarch
2 Tbsp. soy sauce
1 - 2 Tbsp. vinegar
1/2 cup water
1 - 2 green peppers, diced

Method:
Combine beef, crumbs, onions, salt, pepper. Shape into 1 inch balls. Melt shortening then cook meatballs until browned. Drain off drippings and remove meatballs. Combine sugar and cornstarch. Add soy sauce, water, vinegar and pineapple. Cook in fry pan until mixture boils and thickens. (More water may be added.) Add green peppers and meatballs. Simmer 15 - 20 minutes. Serve over rice.

Comment:
Sauce also good with chicken.

Japanese Meat Balls

from Helena McMann, Gold River, B.C.

Ingredients:
- 2 lbs. ground beef
- 4 Tbsp. bread crumbs
- 1 Tsp. salt
- 2 onions
- 1 Tbsp. flour
- 1/4 Tsp. pepper

SAUCE:
- 1 cup brown sugar
- 1/4 Tsp. ginger
- 1 1/2 cups Ketchup
- 1/2 cup soy sauce
- 1 1/2 cups sweet pickle juice

Method:
Mix two eggs into above ingredients. Make into balls. Brown a little. Combine sauce ingredients in saucepan. Bring to boil. Add meat balls. Simmer for 45 minutes.

South African Meat Loaf

from Esperanza Kitchen

Serves 4
Temperature is 375°
Baking time is 45 minutes
Uses a Loaf pan, buttered

Ingredients:
- 2 medium onions
- 2 Tbsp. margarine
- 2 Tbsp. curry
- 1 Tbsp. sugar
- 1/2 cup water
- 1 lb. hamburger
- 2 Tsp. salt
- 1/2 cup raisins or dried apricots
- 1 cup bread-crumbs
- 1 egg
- 1 1/4 cups milk
- butter (optional)

Method:
Slice onions thinly and brown in butter. Add curry, sugar, water and raisins. Cook slowly for 5 minutes. Mix together hamburger, salt, bread-crumbs egg and milk. Put half of hamburger mixture into loaf pan. Cover with onion and curry mixture. Then add remaining hamburger mixture. Bake.

Hot Tamale Pie

from Kathy Harmsworth, Esperanza, B.C.

350°
Baking time is 30 minutes
Uses a 1 1/2 Quart baking dish

Ingredients:

1 cup corn meal
2 cups water
1 Tsp. salt
1 Tbsp. oil
1 lb. ground beef
1/2 cup chopped onion
2 Tbsp. flour
2 Tsp. chili
1 Tsp. salt
pinch garlic
2 cups tomatoes
1/2 cup grated cheese

Method:

Combine corn meal, water and salt and put in bottom of baking dish. Combine ground beef, onion, flour, chili, salt, garlic, tomatoes in oil in pan. Simmer for 10 minutes. Add to corn meal mixture. Bake for 30 minutes. Sprinkle grated cheese on top and bake for 5 - 10 minutes more.

Beef Quickie Pie

from Bernice Bolton, Gold River, B.C.

Temperature is 350°
Baking time is 25 minutes

Ingredients:

2 Tbsp. butter
1 onion chopped
1 lb. ground beef
1 Tbsp. steak sauce
2 cups cooked green beans
1 can tomato soup
mashed potatoes
1 Tsp. salt

Method:

Saute onion until tender. Add ground beef, steak sauce and salt. Brown, stir in soup and beans and pour into casserole. Top with mashed potatoes. Cook.

Tortiere (Fr.Canadian Meat Pie)

from Eleanor Snyder, Edmonton, Alta.

Temperature is 425°
Baking time is 40 minutes
Uses a two 9 inch pie pans

Ingredients:

2 lbs. lean ground pork
1 lb. lean ground beef
2 large onions
1 garlic clove
2 1/2 Tsp. poultry seasoning
2 Tsp. salt
1 Tsp. celery salt
1 1/2 Tsp. pepper
1/2 Tsp. ground sage
1 cup water
3 medium potatoes,
mashed
favourite pastry

Method:

Line pie plates with dough. Fry up meat, onions and spices. Add mashed potatoes. Put mixture in pie plates. Cover with pastry and prick. Bake.

Shipwreck

from Esperanza Kitchen

Serves 5
Temperature is 350-300°
Baking time is 2 hours
Uses a 2 quart casserole

Ingredients:

potatoes, sliced and salted
onions, sliced
1 lb. of hamburger
1/2 cup raw rice
celery, cubed
1 can tomato soup
1 can water

Method:

Put one layer of potatoes in casserole dish, then a layer of the onions, next hamburger layer. Sprinkle rice evenly over this. Then a layer of celery. Over this pour a tin of tomato soup and a can of water. Bake at 350° for the first hour. Turn down to 300° for the second hour.

Bolognese Lasagne

from Marilyn Atleo, Vancouver, B.C.

Makes 8 servings
Temperature is 375°
Baking time is 30 minutes or till hot & bubbly
Uses a 13x9 inch baking dish

Ingredients:

1 1/2 lbs. ground beef
1 minced garlic clove
1 - 15 oz. can tomato sauce
1/2 cup butter or margarine
1/4 Tsp. nutmeg
1/2 cup grated Parmesan cheese
1 large onion diced
1/4 lb. chopped mushrooms
salt and pepper
1/2 cup flour
4 cups milk
1/2 pkg. 16oz. lasagna noodles

Method:

In skillet cook ground beef, onion, garlic till all pan juices evaporate and beef well browned. Stir. Add mushrooms, tomato sauce, salt and pepper. Reduce heat .Simmer uncovered 15 min. Remove Bolognese sauce from heat. In saucepan,low heat melt butter, stir in flour, nutmeg, salt and pepper till blended. Gradually add milk, parmesan cheese. Cook. Stir till thickened. Remove Parmesan sauce. Cook noodles. Layer in dish 1/4 Parmesan sauce, 1/3 noodles, 1/3 Bolognese. Repeat and bake with cheese.

Note: Prepare about 1 1/2 hours before serving.

Lasagne

from Dottie Dale, Seattle, Wash.

Makes 10 - 12 servings
Temperature is 350°
Baking time is 20 - 30 minutes

Ingredients:

1 1/2 lbs. ground beef, browned
1 cup chopped onion
1 large can of tomatoes
1 large can of tomato sauce
1 Tbsp. salt
1 Tsp. pepper
1 Tbsp. parsley flakes
1/2 Tsp. paprika
1 Tsp. chili powder
dash of garlic salt

Cottage Cheese Mixture:
3 beatten eggs
1 lb. cottage cheese, small curd
chopped parsley
bread-crumbs, salt, pepper
Lasagne noodles
Sprinkling 1/4 lb. parmesan or cheddar cheese

Method:

Simmer beef, onion, tomatoes, sauce, salt, pepper, seasonings for half hour. In casserole dish layer the meat sauce, the cottage cheese mixture and cooked lasagne noodles. Then the grated cheese. Finish with meat sauce layer. Sprinkle with grated parmesan cheese. Bake.

Stuffed Meat Loaf

from Kathy Harmsworth, Esperanza, B.C.

Temperature is 375°
Baking time is 35 minutes
Uses a 9 x 6 inch bread pan

Ingredients:

1/2 can (15 oz) tomato
   sauce
1 lb. lean hamburger
1 cup cooked rice
1 egg
1 cup frozen peas or beans
3 - 1 oz slices Mozzarella
   cheese
1/2 Tsp. garlic powder
2 Tbsp. chopped parsley
2 Tbsp. grated Parmesan
1/2 Tsp. salt
1/4 Tsp. pepper

Method:

Measure and set aside 1/2 cup
tomato sauce. Mix remaining ingredients in large bowl. Shape half of
mixture into bread pan. Arrange
three 1 - oz. slices Mozzarella cheese
on top. Sprinkle with peas. Press
remaining beef mixture over filling
and seal edges completely to form
smooth loaf. Pour reserved half cup
tomato sauce on top. Bake. Let set at
least 5 minutes before trying to remove to platter. Otherwise it falls
apart.

Cabbage - Hamburger Casserole

from Jo Carter, Nebraska

Temperature is 350°
Baking time is 30 minutes
Uses a Large shallow pan

Ingredients:

1 medium head of cabbage
1 lb. ground beef
1 cup sour cream
1 cup grated cheddar
   cheese
salt
pepper
bread crumbs

Method:

Steam coarsley sliced cabbage till
tender but crisp. Drain. Brown beef
and leave in quite large chunks.
Add cabbage to meat. Combine sour
cream, cheese, salt and pepper. Stir
into cabbage and meat. Spread in
pan. Cover with bread crumbs
mixed with a little more grated
cheese. Bake.

Beef and Noodle Casserole

from Lois Hooks, Edmonton, Alta.

Temperature is 350°
Baking time is 30 - 50 minutes

Ingredients:
2 cups raw tiny shell
  macaroni
2 lb. hamburger
1 large onion chopped
1 can cream of mushroom
  soup
1 can cream of chicken
  soup
1 cup cheddar cheese soup
1 can water
salt/pepper
TOPPING:
1 cup bread-crumbs
chopped parsley
1/4 cup margarine
paprika

Method:
Cook and drain macaroni. Saute
meat and onions. Add soup and all
other ingredients. Put in large
casserole and sprinkle topping over.

Zucchini Casserole

from Cathy Birtles, Calgary, Alta.

Temperature is 375°
Baking time is 30 minutes

Ingredients:
2 lbs. zucchini, washed/
  sliced
3 Tbsp. chopped onion
2 cups stewed tomatoes
1 Tsp. oregano
1/2 Tsp. salt
pepper
1 cup cooked rice or
1 cup hamburger
3 Tbsp. butter
cheese

Method:
Saute zucchini and onion in butter.
Mash and add the tomatoes to the
zucchini. Cook for 5 minutes. Add
seasonings. Then add the rice or
hamburger or both. Place in casserole dish and sprinkle with cheese.
Bake.

Potato and Hamburger Casserole

from Ruth Sadler, Tofino, B.C.

Serves 6
Temperature is 350°
Baking time is 1 1/2 hours

Ingredients:
- 1 lb. hamburger
- 1 onion, sliced
- 1 can of cream of mushroom soup
- 6 potatoes (approx.)
- salt
- pepper

Method:
Brown hamburger and sliced onions. Add salt and pepper. Pour off any fat. Slice potatoes. Place in layer in bottom of casserole. Place hamburger mixture. Cover with sliced potatoes. Mix mushroom soup with 1/3 can of water. Pour over potato mixture. Cover and bake for 1 hour. Remove the lid for the last half hour.

Mock Enchilada Pie

from Lou & Dale Harris, Union Bay, B.C.

Serves 6
Temperature is 350°
Baking time is 30 minutes

Ingredients:
- 1 chopped garlic clove
- 4 Tbsp. flour
- 1 small can chili sauce
- salt/pepper
- 1 lb. hamburger
- 1 large onion, chopped
- 1 bell pepper, chopped
- small can chopped olives
- 1 Tsp. chili powder
- 1 can chili beans (optional)
- Grated cheese
- Corn chips

Method:
Fry together the first ten ingredients. Alternate layers of this with layer of grated cheese, then layer of crushed corn chips. Repeat so that there are two layers of each in casserole. Bake.

Italian Pizza

from Esperanza Kitchen

Serves 12
Temperature is 450°
Baking time is 12 - 15 minutes
Uses a 12 x 13 inch pan

Ingredients:
- 6 - 8 sausages or weiners
- 1 can spaghetti sauce or tomato juice
- 1/2 Tsp. oregano
- 1/3 Tsp. pepper
- 1 lb. Mozzarella cheese
- 1 cup cooked mushrooms
- 1/4 cup green peppers
- 6 - 8 olives
- 1/3 cup chopped onions
- 1 Tsp. salt

CRUST:
- 2/3 cup of lukewarm water
- 1 Tsp. sugar
- 1 env. dry yeast
- 2 1/4 cups bisquick mix

Method:
Combine water, sugar, yeast. Stir in enough bisquick to make soft but firm dough. Slightly knead. Then press into pan. Arrange other ingredients on dough. Bake.

Note: See Bisquick recipe for making the crust on page 11

Laurel's Pizza Crust

from Lorraine Ennis, Ucluelet, B.C.

Ingredients:
- 1 3/4 cups flour
- 2 Tsp. baking powder
- 5 Tbsp. oil
- 3/4 cup milk

Method:
Combine all ingredients and press into pizza pan. Top with tomato sauce and spices or spaghetti sauce, Parmesam cheese, mozzarella and favourite toppings. Doubles well. Pizzas may be made several hours ahead of time and refrigerated.

Sausage - Sweet Potato Bake

from Merle Hagerty, Gold River, B.C.

Temperature is 375°
Baking time is 50 - 60 minutes
Uses a 2 qt. casserole

Ingredients:
1 lb. bulk pork sausage
2 med. raw sweet potatoes
2 Tbsp. sugar
3 medium apples
1/4 Tsp. ground cinna-
mon
1/4 Tsp. salt
1/2 cup water
1 Tbsp. flour

Method:
Brown and drain sausage meat.
(Break up large pieces.) Peel and
slice potatoes and apples. Arrange
in casserole. Combine sugar, flour,
cinnamon, salt and water and pour
over the top of first mixture. Bake.

Liz's Sausage Casserole

from Esperanza Kitchen

Serves 4
Temperature is 350°
Baking time is 60 minutes

Ingredients:
1 lb. sausage
1 stalk celery
1 can tomato soup
1 Tsp. brown sugar
1 large onion
1/2 cup rice
1 can warm water

Method:
Place chopped onion and celery on
bottom of casserole dish. Spread rice
evenly on top. Place sausages over
rice. Pour soup and water and
brown sugar over rice. Bake.

Pork Hawaiian

from Audrey Dol, Tahsis, B.C.

Ingredients:
1 egg
2 Tbsp. water
1/4 cup flour
1/4 Tsp. salt
2 cups cubed pork
3 Tbsp. shortening
1-13 1/2 oz can pineapple
   tidbits
juice from pineapple
   tidbits
2 Tbsp. vinegar
2 Tbsp. soy sauce
1 med. pepper cut in strips
1-15oz can water chestnuts
1-3oz can sliced mush-
   rooms
1 Tbsp. cornstarch

Method:
Beat egg thoroughly. Add water, flour and salt. Beat until smooth. Stir in meat mixing until coated. Melt shortening in medium skillet. Add meat mixture, cook and stir till meat is brown. Remove from heat, keep warm. Blend cornstarch, pineapple juice, vinegar, soy sauce in saucepan. Cook and stir till mixture thickens and boils. Boil for 1 min. Stir in pineapple, green pepper, chestnuts, mushrooms. Cook till pepper is tender. Stir in meat. Heat well.

Bar-B-Qued Spare Ribs

from Darlene Streiker, Tahsis, B.C.

Temperature is 325°
Baking time is 2 hours

Ingredients:
spare ribs
salt
pepper
garlic
1 1/4 cups Ketchup
1 1/4 cups water
1 medium onion, chopped
1 1/2 Tsp. mustard
1 1/2 Tsp. Worcestershire
   sauce
1/4 cup brown sugar

Method:
Brown spare ribs in frying pan with salt, pepper, garlic. Drain off fat before adding sauce. Boil together Ketchup, water, onion, mustard, Worcestershire sauce and brown sugar for 10 minutes. Then add to ribs and bake.

Pork Chops with Rice

from Ruby Quiring, Regina, Sask.

Temperature is 350°
Baking time is 1 1/2 hours

Ingredients:
6 pork chops
3 Tbsp. shortening
1 cup rice
salt
pepper
3 onions
1 can mushroom soup
1 green pepper
1 can water

Method:
Melt shortening and brown chops well on both sides. Wash rice and sprinkle over chops. add chopped onions and green pepper, mushroom soup, salt and pepper. Cover closely and cook for 1 1/2 hours. Adding water, if necessary, so rice will not be dry.

Sweet & Sour Pork Chops

from Lorna Penner, Kyuquot, B.C.

Temperature is 375°
Baking time is 1 1/2 hours

Ingredients:
6 pork steaks
1 cup water
1 cup brown sugar
1/2 cup vinegar
2 Tbsp. Worcestershire
   sauce
1/2 cup Ketchup
1 large onion
1 cup chopped celery
1 or 2 eggs
bread crumbs

Method:
Beat eggs. Salt and pepper steaks. Dip in egg and coat with bread crumbs. Brown on both sides. Put in covered roasting pan. Brown onion and celery. Prepare sauce quickly by bringing above ingredients to boil. Thicken with cornstarch (not too thick). Pour over steaks in pan. Top with onions and celery. When cooking well, turn heat down to 300° and continue to bake. Serve with rice and lettuce salad.

Veal and Mushrooms

from Esperanza Kitchen

Serves 6

Ingredients:

3 Tbsp. soy sauce
2 lbs. lean veal, cubed
2 onions, diced
1 clove garlic, minced
1 cup water, stock or
  tomato juice
1/4 Tsp. sugar substitute
1/2 Tsp. salt to taste
1/2 Tsp. pepper to taste
1 Tsp. rosemary or marjo-
  ram
2 small carrots, sliced thin
4 large green peppers,
  chopped
2 small cans mushrooms
1 Tsp. grated lemon rind
water

Method:

Measure soy sauce into large non-stick skillet, brown veal, onions and garlic on medium heat. Stir often for 15 minutes. Add water and seasonings. Cook, covered, until veal is tender (low heat) about 1 hour. Fifteen minutes before done add carrots, green peppers, mushrooms. Just before serving stir in rind. Add water as necessary.

Notes

Spanish Liver

from Esperanza Kitchen

Temperature is 350°
Baking time is 25 - 30 minutes

Ingredients:
- 1 lb. liver
- 3 Tbsp. fat
- 2 Tbsp. brown sugar
- 2 Tbsp. Ketchup
- 1/2 Tsp. dry mustard
- 1 Tsp. paprika
- 1 Tbsp. Worcestershire
- 1/4 Tsp. chili sauce
- 1 cup canned tomatoes
- 1 medium onion sliced
- 1 green pepper sliced
- 2 Tbsp. flour

Method:
Dip liver in seasoned flour. Brown in fat. Place in casserole dish. Combine in bowl the flour, sugar, ketchup, mustard, paprika, Worcester- shire sauce, chili powder and tomatoes. Pour mixture over liver. Arrange sliced onions and green peppers over top. Cover and bake for 15 minutes then uncover and bake 10 - 15 minutes longer.

Venison Pot Roast

from Nadine Kruger, Campbell River, B.C.

Ingredients:
- 8 lb. venison roast
- 1/4 lb. salt pork (bacon)
- 1/4 cup butter
- 3 medium onions
- 2 bay leaves
- 1 clove garlic
- 3 large carrots
- 2 1/2 cups vegetable stock
- 1/4 Tsp. allspice
- 4 Tbsp. honey
- 4 fillets anchovy (optional)
- 2 Tbsp. flour
- 1/2 cup vinegar
- 2 cups heavy or sour cream
- salt & pepper

Method:
Rub roast with pork. Brown roast in big stewing pot with butter. Add onions, bay leaves, garlic, carrots, hot vegetable stock, allspice, honey, anchovies (mashed in a cup with vinegar), salt, pepper. Bring to boil. Simmer on low heat for 2 - 2 1/2 hours. Strain stock and return to pot. Stir in cream and flour mixture. Return roast. Simmer 5 to 10 minutes. Stir in vinegar before serving.

Impossible Quiche

from Vera Stewart, Haiti

Temperature is 350°
Baking time is 45 minutes
Uses a 9 inch pie pan, buttered

Ingredients:

3 eggs
1/2 cup Bisquick mix
1 1/2 cups milk
salt/pepper
1 cup grated cheese
ham/bacon/shrimp/etc.

Method:

Combine first four ingredients in blender and then pour into pie plate. Sprinkle meat and cheese on top and push below surface with back of spoon.

Note: See Bisquick recipe on page 11

Paprika Beef

from Lois Hooks, Edmonton, Alberta

Makes 6 to 8 servings
Cooking time is 2 - 2 1/2 hours

Ingredients:

1/4 cup shortening
2 lb. beef chuck cut in 1 inch cube
1 cup sliced onion
1 sm. clove garlic, minced
3/4 cup Ketchup
2 Tbsp. Worcestershire sauce
1 Tbsp. brown sugar
2 Tsp. salt
2 Tsp. paprika
1/2 Tsp. dry mustard
1 1/2 cups water
2 Tbsp. flour
1/4 cup water
3 cups cooked noodles

Method:

Melt shortening in large skillet. Add meat, onion and garlic. Cook and stir till meat is brown and onion tender. Add all other ingredients except for flour, 1/4 cup water and noodles. Cover and simmer for 2 - 2 1/2 hours. Blend flour and 1/4 cup water. Gradually stir into meat mixture. Heat to boiling. Stir constantly. Boil and stir 1 minute. Serve over noodles.

Pizza Buns

from Camp Ferrier

Broil till bubbly

Ingredients:
- 1 lb. bologna, chopped
- 1 chopped onion
- 1 chopped green pepper
- 3 stalks celery, chopped
- 1/2 lb. Cheeze Whiz or grated cheese
- 1 - 10 oz tin tomato soup
- buns

Method:
Fry bologna, drain and set aside. Fry onion, green pepper and celery. Add bologna, cheese and tomato soup. Put on buns and broil till bubbly.

Pizza Spread for Buns

from Esperanza Kitchen

Ingredients:
- 2 tins prem, weiners or sausage
- 1 - 10 oz. can tomato soup
- 2 diced onions
- 1 lb. diced Mozzarella or process cheese
- 1 lb. bacon (optional)
- 1 green pepper
- 1 can (6 oz) tomato paste
- 1 Tsp. garlic salt
- 1/4 Tsp. oregano
- 1/8 lb. pepperoni, salami, etc.

Method:
In frying pan saute onions and green pepper. Add tomato soup, tomato paste, garlic salt, and oregano. Spread warm mixture on buns. Top with preferred meat and sprinkle with mozzarella or process cheese. Broil at 450°.

Green Pepper Steak

from Shelly Jones, Payson, Arkansas

Ingredients:
- 1 lb. beef chuck or round, fat trimmed
- 1/4 cup soy sauce
- 1 clove garlic
- 1 1/2 Tsp. grated fresh ginger or 1/2 Tsp. ground ginger
- 1/4 cup salad oil
- 1 cup green onion thinly sliced
- 1 cup 1 inch cut green/red peppers
- 2 stalks celery thinly sliced
- 1 Tbsp. cornstarch
- 1 cup water
- 2 tomatoes cut into wedges

Method:
With very sharp knife cut beef cross grain into thin strips. Combine soy sauce, garlic, ginger. Add beef. Toss. Set aside. Prepare vegetables. Heat oil in large frying pan or wok. Add beef and toss over high heat till browned. Taste meat. If not tender cover and simmer for 30 - 40 min. over low heat. Turn heat up add vegetables. Toss until they are crisp, about 10 minutes. Mix cornstarch with water. Add to pan. Cook till thickened. Add tomatoes. Heat.

Sauce for Peameal Bacon

from Fanny Carlile, Victoria, B.C.

Baking time is 2 hours

Ingredients:
- 1 lb. peameal bacon
- 1/2 cup brown sugar
- 1 Tsp. dry mustard
- 2 Tbsp. corn syrup
- 1 Tbsp. vinegar

Method:
Mix sugar, mustard and vinegar. Put bacon in dutch oven or heavy fry pan with lid. Pour sauce over meat. Cover, bake slowly until cooked.

Casseroles, Salads, Soups and other good stuff

Shantyman Sandwich

from Percy Wills and Harold Peters

Ingredients:
- bread
- butter
- mayonnaise
- peanut butter
- juicy orange
- juicy spanish onion

Method:
Generously butter two slices of bread. Carefully spread just the right amount of mayonnaise on one slice. Generously spread peanut butter on the other slice. With a sharp knife peel and finely slice a juicy orange and peel and finely slice a juicy spanish onion. Place the orange on the peanut butter slice. Place the onion on the mayonnaise slice. Put the two together. A mouth watering delicious sandwich. You'll enjoy it.

Note:
West Coast salmon added to this sandwich is delicious, Percy and Harold tell us. As pioneer Shantymen missionaries aboard The Messenger II and Messenger III, they served this sandwich to many guests.

Pizza Burger

from Marlene Scott, Campbell River, B.C.

Ingredients:
- 1 can (14 oz.) tomato sauce
- 1/2 cup oil
- 1 tin mushroom pieces
- 1/4 lb. grated cheese
- 1 small onion, chopped
- 1/4 Tsp. garlic
- 1 Tsp. salt
- 1 Tsp. pepper
- 1 Tsp. oregano

Method:
Mix all ingredients together. Spread on buns and put in oven for 10 - 12 minutes till cheese melts.

Comment: Can be made ahead of time and stored in fridge.

Baked Beans

from Esperanza Kitchen

Ingredients:

1 lb. navy beans
2 qts. water
1/2 cup molasses
1/2 cup Ketchup
1 Tsp. mustard
2 Tsp. salt
1/4 Tsp. pepper
2 slices of chopped bacon
    or 1/4 lb. of salt pork
1 chopped onion (op-
    tional)

Method:

Soak beans in water overnight. In same liquid bring beans to a boil. Simmer until tender. Pour into a bean pot or casserole dish or crock pot. Add remaining ingredients. Stir occasionally. Additional water may be needed. Simmer all day.

Refried Beans

from Coastal Missions

Ingredients:

1 pound dry pinto beans
    (2 1/2 cups)
6 cups water
1/4 cup bacon drippings
1 1/2 Tsp. salt
1 clove garlic
1/2 cup chopped onion
1/2 cup Ketchup (op-
    tional)
Tabasco sauce
sliced green onion
grated cheddar cheese

Method:

Bring beans and water to boil. Simmer for 3 hours or till beans are soft. In a large skillet melt bacon drippings. Add beans with liquid, salt and garlic. Mash beans completely. Add chopped onion. Cook at medium heat about 10 minutes, stirring often. Add Tabasco if desired or Ketchup before serving. When ready to serve add grated cheddar cheese and sliced green onion.

Schwawties Hash Browns

from Nadine Kruger, Campbell River, B.C.

Temperature is 350°
Cooking time is 1 - 1 1/2 hrs
Uses a 9x13 buttered dish

Ingredients:

2 lbs. hash browns frozen
  or fresh
2 cups sour cream
2 tins cream of mushroom
  soup
1/2 cup melted butter
grated onion
salt
2 cups grated cheddar
  cheese
parmesan cheese

Method:

Thaw potatoes. Mix first six ingredients in baking dish. Sprinkle with parmesan cheese on top. Put in oven.

Fred's Breakfast Potatoes

from Esperanza Kitchen

Uses an electric or heavy skillet

Ingredients:

3 slices bacon
8 cups boiled potatoes
1/2 cup chopped onions
1/4 cup chopped green
  pepper
1/2 cup cheddar cheese
  (optional)
4 eggs
1/4 cup milk
salt/pepper

Method:

Chop or slice potatoes. Grate cheese. Fry bacon until crisp. Set aside and drain off most of fat. Into 3 tbsps. of drippings add onion and green pepper, saute slightly. Add potatoes, salt/pepper. While potatoes are frying. In a separate bowl beat 4 eggs well. Add milk and cheese. Reduce heat under potatoes when browned. Add egg mixture. Cover pan. Cook until eggs are done. Turning gently. Crumble bacon on top.

Pyrogies

from Donna Paracy, Tahsis, B.C.

Ingredients:
5 1/2 cups flour
4 eggs
1 pinch soda
1 1/2 Tsp. baking powder
1 Tbsp. salt
1 1/2 cups milk

Method:
Combine all ingredients and work till smooth. Cutting one piece at a time, roll thin and fill with one of the following fillings. Fold over and pinch edges securely. Boil about 6 at a time until done. Transfer to a pan of fried onions in butter.

Filling for Pyrogies - #1

from Donna Paracy, Tahsis, B.C.

Ingredients:
onions
sauerkraut
butter
mashed potatoes

Method:
Fry onions and sauerkraut in butter. Mix with mashed potatoes. Fill pyrogies.

Filling for Pyrogies - #2

from Donna Paracy, Tahsis, B.C.

Ingredients:
Grated cheddar cheese
mashed potatoes

Method:
Mix together cheese and mashed potatoes. Fill pyrogies.

Filling for Pyrogies - #3

from Donna Paracy, Tahsis, B.C.

Ingredients:
1 cup cottage cheese
salt to taste
1 egg yolk
1 cup mashed potatoes

Method:
Mix all ingredients together and fill pyrogies.

Luncheon Cheese Puff

from Helen Ottom, Campbell River, B.C.

Serves 6
Temperature is 325°
Baking time is 60 minutes approx.
Uses a 12 x 18 inch baking dish

Ingredients:
12 slices bread
1/2 lb. sliced cheese
4 eggs
1/2 Tsp. dry mustard
2 1/2 cups milk
1/4 Tsp. onion seasoning
dash of red pepper
1/2 Tsp. salt

Method:
Trim crusts from bread and make 6
cheese sandwiches. Arrange in
bottom of a baking dish. Cut sandwiches to fit pan if necessary. Beat
eggs slightly, add milk and seasonings and pour over the sandwiches.
Cover with wax paper and refrigerate for one hour. Bake for one hour
or until knife inserted in centre
comes out clean.

Comment:
Give yourself 2 hours to prepare this dish. A good lunch dish, add a
salad and you will have a complete meal.

Rice and Broccoli Casserole

from Colleen Shonwise, Tahsis, B.C.

Temperature is 350°
Baking time is 30 - 40 minutes
Uses a buttered baking dish

Ingredients:
1 cup cooked rice
1 large head broccoli,
  chopped
1 large onion, chopped
2 Tbsp. butter
1 can cream of chicken
  soup
3/4 cup milk
1/2 lb. grated cheese

Method:
Saute onions in butter. Heat soup,
milk and cheese together until
cheese is melted. Mix all ingredients
and turn into baking dish. Bake.

Macaroni and Cheese

from Esperanza Kitchen

Serves 4
Temperature is 375°
Baking time is 30 minutes
Uses a 1 1/2 - 2 quart greased casserole dish

Ingredients:
1 cup macaroni
1/4 cup margarine
1 Tbsp. chopped onion
1/4 cup flour
1/2 Tsp. salt
1/4 Tsp. dry mustard
dash pepper
2 cups milk
1 cup grated cheddar
cheese
2/3 cup buttered bread-
crumbs

Method:
Cook macaroni in salted water.
Drain. Melt margarine. Add
chopped onion. Cook slowly until
tender but not brown. Blend in
flour, salt, dry mustard, pepper.
Gradually stir in milk. Cook constantly until thickened. Add cheese.
Pour over cooked macaroni.
Sprinkle with buttered bread-
crumbs. Bake. (Can be multiplied.)

Vegetable Quiche Pie

from Dorthea McLean, Surrey, B.C.

Temperature is 400°
Baking time is 35 - 40 minutes
Uses a lightly greased pie plate

Ingredients:
2 cups chopped broccoli
or cauliflower
1/2 cup onion diced
1/2 cup diced green
pepper
1 cup grated cheddar
cheese
1 1/2 cups milk
3/4 cup bisquick mix
(page 11)
3 eggs
1 Tsp. salt
1/4 Tsp. pepper

Method:
Heat to boiling 1/2 Tsp salt to 1 cup
water. Add broccoli. Cover and heat
to boiling. Cook till near tender. 5
min. Drain. Mix broccoli, onion,
green pepper and cheese in plate.
Beat remaining ingredients till
smooth and pour into pie plate. Bake
until golden brown when knife
inserted in comes out clean.

Savoury Cheese & Onion Flan

from Doris Kreller, Errington, B.C.

Temperature is 400°
Baking time is 35 - 40 minutes
Uses a 10 inch flan pan

Ingredients:

BASE:
- 1/2 cup whole wheat flour
- 1/4 cup margarine
- pinch of salt
- water

FILLING:
- 1/2 cup grated cheddar
- 2 Tbsp. whole wheat flour
- 2 large onions, chopped
- oil
- 4 large firm tomatoes, sliced
- 3 large eggs
- 3/4 cup milk
- 1/4 cup whole wheat bread crumbs
- pinch of nutmeg
- 1 Tsp. basil
- salt
- pepper

Method:

Base:
Rub margarine into flour, salt. Add enough water to make a soft, fairly wet dough. Roll out, line flan pan.

Filling:
Toss cheese, flour in bowl. Saute onions in oil till golden. Spread 1/3 of cheese, flour mixture over pastry lined pan. Arrange onions on this. Heat tomatoes gently with basil in oil 1 min. Arrange slices over onions. Cover with rest of cheese/flour mix.Beat eggs, milk, salt & pepper. Pour over. Sprinkle breadcrumbs and nutmeg on top.

Greek Salad

from Isabel McPherson, Whitby, Ont.

Ingredients:
- 2 tomatoes, cut bite size
- 1 cucumber, cut bite size
- 1/4 cup green onion, sliced
- 1/2 cup ripe olives, sliced
- 3/4 cup Feta cheese, cubed
- 1/2 cup olive oil
- 1/4 cup red wine vinegar
- 1/4 cup chopped parsley
- 1/2 Tsp. pepper
- 1/8 Tsp. oregano
- 1/8 Tsp. garlic

Method:
Combine all ingredients.

Raw Onion Salad

from Lorna Penner, Kyuquot, B.C.

Serves 6 - 12

Ingredients:
- 4 big Spanish onions
- 3/4 cup vinegar
- 3/4 cup water
- 3/4 cup white sugar
- 1 Tsp. celery seed
- Salad dressing (Miracle Whip)

Method:
Peel and cut onions in thin slices. Soak in vinegar, water and sugar solution overnight. Come morning - drain well and add salad dressing and 1 teaspoon celery seed. Mix well and put in fridge till ready to use. (Chill well.)

Coleslaw

from Esperanza Kitchen

Serves 10

Ingredients:
- 1 large cabbage, shredded fine
- 2 large onions, thinly sliced

DRESSING:
- 3/4 cup sugar
- 1 Tsp. salt
- 1 cup white vinegar
- 2 Tsp. mustard
- 1/4 cup sugar
- 3 Tsp. celery seed
- 3/4 cup oil

Method:
Pour 3/4 cup sugar over vegetables. Combine rest of ingredients and boil for 5 minutes. Pour dressing over vegetables. Cool 3 - 4 hours.

Sauerkraut Salad

from Elsie Lindholm, Camrose, Alta.

Ingredients:
- 1 cup green pepper
- 1 cup celery
- 1 cup onion
- 1/2 cup salad oil
- 1/2 cup vinegar
- 14 oz. can sauerkraut
- scant cup of sugar

Method:
Drain and cut sauerkraut. Cut pepper, onion and celery fine. Mix all ingredients together. Will keep for sometime in refrigerator.

Cabbage and Fruit Salad

from Bonnie Ebel, Abbotsford, B.C.

Serves 6

Ingredients:
1 small tin orange sections
2 apples, chopped
2 cups shredded cabbage
1 cup seedless grapes
DRESSING:
1/2 cup whipping cream
1 Tbsp. sugar
1 Tbsp. lemon juice
1/2 cup mayonnaise

Method:
Place oranges, apples, cabbage and grapes in bowl. Whip cream. Fold in sugar, lemon juice and mayonnaise. Stir into fruit mixture.

Carrot Pineapple Jello Salad

from Marion McLean

Uses an 8x13 pyrex dish

Ingredients:
1 large pkg. orange jello
1 - 14oz. can crushed pine-
    apple
1 1/2 cups grated carrots
1/3 - 1/2 cup walnuts,
    chopped

Method:
Mix jello according to package directions except decrease cold water to 1 3/4 cup. Drain pineapple and add fruit to jello. Chill till beginning to set. Peel and grate carrots. Chop nuts finely. Add to partially set jello and set in 8x13 pyrex dish. When set cut in squares and put a dab of mayonnaise and sprig of parsley in centre of each square.

Jello Salad

from Alma Cunningham, Victoria, B.C.

Ingredients:
- 1 pkg. lemon or line jello
- 1 cup boiling water
- 1/2 cup Miracle Whip
- 1 cup grated cheese
- 1 can crushed pineapple

Method:
Dissolve jello in boiling water. Add Miracle Whip, cheese and pineapple. Mix well and let set.

Yum, Yum Sour Cream Fruit Salad

from Cy Lazell, Victoria, B.C.

Ingredients:
- 1 can fruit cocktail
- 1 can Mandarin orange segments
- 1 can pineapple chunks or tidbits
- 1 large apple, pared, cored, diced
- 1 heaping cup minature marshmallows
- 2 heaping Tbsp. Miracle Whip

Method:
Combine all ingredients and mix well.

Comment:
This is not a dessert but is to be eaten with main course.

164

Green Jello Salad

from Kay Good, Coquitlam, B.C.

Ingredients:
- 1-14 oz. can of pears
- 8 oz. cream cheese (room temp.)
- 6 oz. lime jello
- 1/2 pt. whipping cream (whipped)

Method:
Drain pears and mash. Heat juice to boiling adding water to make one cup. Add jello powder to dissolve. While still on heat add cream cheese to dissolve. Remove from heat. Chill and whip cream. Fold into jello mixture crushed pears and whipped cream. Allow to set two hours. Decorate with parsley and cherry.

Sister Accier Salad

from Marion McLean

Ingredients:
- 1 cup sour cream
- 1 cup long shredded coconut
- 1 cup mandarin oranges, drained
- 1 cup pineapple, drained
- 1 cup marshmallows, quartered

Method:
Mix all ingredients together and refrigerate a day before serving.

Comment:
This is delicious served with turkey, chicken and all roasts.

Lime Jello

from Alma Cunningham, Victoria, B.C.

Ingredients:
- 1 - 3 oz. pkg. lime jello powder
- 1 cup boiling water
- 1 cup cottage cheese
- 1 cup mayonnaise (or less)
- 1/2 cup walnuts
- 1/2 cup crushed pine-apple

Method:
Add boiling water to jello and let cool. Add rest of ingredients and chill.

Eggnog Jello Salad

from Dorthea McLean, Surrey, B.C.

Ingredients:
- 1 double pkg. lemon jello
- 1 cup boiling water
- 2 1/2 cups egg nog

Method:
Dissolve jello in boiling water. Let cool slightly then add egg nog. Pour into mold and allow to set. Decorate.

Comment: Good one for Christmas.

California Salad

from Donna Paracy, Tahsis, B.C.

Ingredients:
- 1 cup white miniature marshmallows
- 1 can pineapple chunks, drained
- 1 can Mandarin oranges, drained
- 1 cup flaked coconut
- 1 cup sour cream

Method:
Combine all ingredients and refrigerate for at least four hours before serving. Stir before serving.

Real Good Salad Dressing

from Edith Gibson, Victoria, B.C.

Ingredients:
- 3/4 cup white sugar
- 6 Tsp. dry mustard
- 1 Tsp. salt
- 2 Tbsp. flour
- 3 eggs, beaten
- 1 cup white vinegar
- 1 cup water

Method:
Mix the four dry ingredients together in a pot. Beat eggs and add to dry ingredients. Add vinegar. Mix well. Then add one cup of boiling water stir until cooked. Store in jar in fridge when cool. If too thick cut it down with lemon juice or vinegar.

Orange-Cream Fruit Salad

from Emilie Patton, Vancouver, B.C.

Serves 10

Ingredients:

1 20-oz. can pineapple
   tidbits,drained
1 16-oz. can peach slices,
   drained
1 11-oz. can mandarin
   orange sections,
drained
3 medium bananas, sliced
2 medium apples, cored
   and chopped
1 – 3 3/4 or 3 5/8 oz. pkg.
   instant vanilla pudding
   mix
1 1/2 cups milk
1/2 of 6 oz.can or 1/3 cup
   frozen
orange juice concentrate,
   thawed
3/4 cup dairy sour cream,
lettuce cups

Method:

In large bowl, combine fruits, set
aside. In small bowl, combine dry
pudding mix, milk and orange juice
concentrate. Beat with rotary beater
till blended, 1-2 minutes. Beat in
sour cream. Fold into fruit mixture.
Cover and chill. Serve in lettuce
cups. Garnish with additional
mandarin oranage sections, if
desired.

Comment:

Add bananas just before serving. When in season strawberries,
peaches, seedles grapes, etc. may be used.

Carrington Bean Dip

from Coastal Missions

Temperature is 450°
Baking time is till heated & cheese melted
Uses a shallow baking dish

Ingredients:
- 17 oz. refried beans
- 8 oz. cream cheese
- 8 oz. sour cream
- 1 pkg. Taco seasoning
- 1/2 cup sliced green onion
- 20 drops Tabassco sauce
- 8 oz. shredded Monterey Jack
- 8 oz. shredded cheddar

Method:
Mix first six ingredients in a large bowl with electric mixer. Pour into ungreased shallow baking dish. Cover with shredded cheese. Bake. (Can also be heated in microwave Power 5 for 10 - 15 minutes.) This dip is good with a group. Corn chips or homemade tortillas dip well. Goes well with all Mexican dishes. Can also be used as a stuffing for enchiladas.

Vegetable Dip

from Colleen Shonwise, Tahsis, B.C.

Ingredients:
- 2/3 cup mayonnaise
- 2/3 cup sour cream
- 1 Tbsp. dry green onions
- 1 Tbsp. parsley flakes
- 1 Tsp. dill weed
- 1 Tsp. seasoning salt
- 1/2 Tsp. Worcestershire sauce
- 1 Tsp. Accent
- 1 drop Tabasco sauce

Method:
Blend all together and serve as a dip for raw vegetables.

Chip Dip Blue Cheese

from Kay Good, Coquitlam, B.C.

Ingredients:
- 1/2 lb. cream cheese
- 1/2 lb. Blue cheese
- 2 Tbsp. grated onion
- 1 Tbsp. prepared horse-radish
- 1/2 cup mayonnaise
- 3 Tbsp. lemon juice

Method:
Have all ingredients at room temperature. Mix all ingredients together. Serve.

Tabooley

from Bonnie Ebel, Abbotsford, B.C.

Serves 6

Ingredients:
- 3/4 cup cracked wheat, bulger
- 1 cup snipped parsley
- 3 medium tomatoes, chopped
- 1/2 cup chopped green onions

Method:
Cover wheat in hot water and soak for half hour. Drain. Combine all ingredients in a bowl and cover with the following Dressing recipe. Salad must sit in fridge for at least three hours before serving.

Tabooley Dressing

from Bonnie Ebel, Abbotsford, B.C.

Ingredients:
- 1/4 cup Golden Italian Dressing
- 1/4 cup vinegar
- 1/3 cup sugar
- 1 1/2 Tbsp. oil
- salt/pepper

Method:
Combine all ingredients together and shake well.

Suggestions for Soups

from Esperanza Kitchen

Ingredients:
 Ketchup
 mustard
 dried soup base
 onion soup mix
 spring vegetable soup mix
 can of tomatoes
dash of Tabasco sauce

Method:
If more zap is needed in a homemade soup add one of these ingredients.

Vegetable Soup Stock

from Esperanza Kitchen

Ingredients:
 2 carrots, shredded
 2 parsnips, shredded
 1/2 large turnip
 4 potatoes
 2 onions, sliced
 3 stalks celery, sliced in
  1/2 in.
 1 onion, minced
 3 qts. water (or pot liq-
  uors)
 1 bay leaf
 2 cups canned tomatoes
 2 Tsp. salt
 1/8 Tsp. pepper
 butter to taste

Method:
Heat water and add vegetables and
bay leaf. Cook uncovered until a full
rolling boil is reached. Cover,
reduce heat and simmer gently for
20 minutes, just until root vegetables
are almost tender. Add cut up
canned tomatoes and cook 5 minutes longer. Then add salt/pepper
and butter.

Comment: Cool stock uncovered, or it may spoil.

Beef Soup Stock

from Esperanza Kitchen

Ingredients:

5 lb. bones
water
1/4 Tsp. pepper or 4
  peppercorns
1 Tsp. salt
1 quartered carrot
4 stalks celery and leaves
4 sprigs of parsley
sprig marjoram (or a
  pinch)
1 sprig of thyme
1 bay leaf

Method:

Sear any meat to be used. Add water to bones. Cover and let come to a boil. Reduce heat and simmer over low heat two or three hours. Half an hour before done - add vegetables. Cool uncovered and then chill in fridge. When cold skim fat which has solidified on top. Remove bones. Use as base for vegetable soup.

Note: 1 pint of water to each pound of meat and bones.

Turkey Soup

from Esperanza Kitchen

Serves 8

Ingredients:

2 quarts of water
turkey bones
1/2 cup shredded celery
  leaves
4 sprigs of parsley
2 sliced onions
2 carrots grated
3 stalks celery sliced
salt/pepper
3/4 cup brown rice
2 cups canned corn (op-
  tional)

Method:

Put bones in cold water to cover. Add celery leaves, parsley, onions, carrots, celery stalks, salt and pepper. Simmer until a rich full flavour is reached about one hour. Strain and add brown rice. Season to taste and simmer until rice is tender - about one hour.Or replace rice with 2 cups canned corn. Simmer just until corn is heated.

Note: Be careful not to boil.

Corn Chowder

from Ruth Steer, Surrey, B.C.

Ingredients:
- 4 strips bacon, diced
- 2/3 cup chopped onion
- 2/3 cup chopped celery
- 5 potatoes, peeled and diced
- 1 can creamed corn
- salt/pepper
- milk

Method:

Cook bacon until crisp along with onions and celery. Cook potatoes in small amount of water. Add bacon, onions, celery, creamed corn, salt and pepper to taste. Add milk to consistency you like. Heat and serve.

Borsch

from Airie Kirby, Campbell River, B.C.

Serves 8

Ingredients:
- 1/4 cup butter
- 1 cup finely chopped onions
- 2 cloves crushed garlic
- 1 lb. potatoes (peeled, chunks)
- 1 lb. coarsely shredded green cabbage
- 2 cups chopped cooked beets
- 1/2 cup chopped celery
- 3 medium tomatoes
- 1 cup parsnips
- 1/2 Tsp. white sugar
- 1/4 cup vinegar
- 1 Tbsp. salt
- 2 qts. beef stock
- 1 1/2 lb. cooked beef
- 1/2 pt. sour cream
- 3 Tbsp. finely chopped dill

Method:

In pan melt butter over moderate heat. Add onions and garlic cook till lightly covered stirring frequently. Peel, seed and coarsely chop tomatoes and peel and chop parsnips. Stir in vegetables, sugar, vinegar, salt and stock. Bring to boil over high heat. Lower heat, partially cover pot. Simmer for 30 min. till potatoes are tender Not Soggy. Add meat. Simmer partially covered 10-15 min. Adjust seasonings. Serve with sour cream sprinkled with dill.

Bow-Tie Noodle Soup

from Val Leong, Tahsis, B.C.

Makes 10 servings

Ingredients:
- 1 pkg. medium bow-tie noodles
- 1 lb. hamburger
- 2 or 3 pkg. chicken noodle soup mix
- dash soy sauce
- fresh vegetables cut up (carrots,etc.)

Method:

Fry hamburger. Prepare vegetables. Put 8 cups water. Bring to boil. Add soup mixes. Then add vegetables. Let boil till vegetables tender. Add noodles and hamburger. Add dash soy sauce. Serve.

Pumpkin Soup

from Vera Stewart, Haiti

Ingredients:
- 1 lb. hamburger
- spices
- onions
- 1 - 10 oz. can pumpkin
- 4 cans water
- 3 medium potates, cubed
- 3 medium carrots, cubed
- (turnip/cabbage/noodles-optional)
- 4 whole allspice
- 8 whole cloves
- diced onion
- garlic/thyme

Method:

Cook pumpkin, potatoes, carrots and any other vegetables in water until soft. Brown hamburger with diced onion. Add spices and meat to vegetables. If too thick add more water. Freeze leftovers.

Comment:

This soup is always served in most Haitian homes the morning of January 1st - their Independence Day. While the Haitians were slaves they were never allowed to have "pumpkin soup" like their owners. So the day of their liberation, January 1st, all the slaves determined to have pumpkin soup and they've had it ever since. Actually their pumpkin is more like Canadian squash.

Fruit Soup

from Karin Hardy, Victoria, B.C.

Ingredients:
1 pkg. mixed dried fruit
1 cup raisins
2 or 3 sticks cinnamon
1/3 cup large tapioca
2 qts. water
1 orange
1 lemon
2 - 3 apples
honey or sugar

Method:
Cut oranges and lemons very thin, rind and all. Add cut up apples (I don't peel them.) and simmer for 20 - 30 minutes. Add any leftover canned fruit or juice. Grape juice is nice. Sweeten to taste with honey or sugar.

Notes

Notes

Basic Cookie Mix

from Jewell Leighton, Duncan, B.C.

Makes 16 cups of mix

Ingredients:
- 8 cups all purpose flour
- 2 1/2 cups granulated sugar
- 2 cups brown sugar, packed
- 4 Tsp. salt
- 1 1/2 Tsp. baking soda
- 3 cups vegetable shortening

Method:
In a large bowl combine dry ingredients. Cut in shortening until evenly distributed. Store in a cool place.

Cookie Recipe from Mix

from Jewell Leighton, Duncan, B.C.

Makes 2 dozen
Temperature is 375°
Baking time is 10 - 15 minutes

Ingredients:
- 3 cups of mix
- 1 Tbsp. milk
- 1 Tsp. vanilla or other choice
- 1 egg
- chocolate chips/nuts/ raisins/etc

Method:
Combine above ingredients. Bake.

Pancake Mix

from Beatrice Sam, Tofino, B.C.

Ingredients:
- 10 cups all-purpose flour
- 2 1/2 cups instant nonfat dry milk
- 1/2 cup sugar
- 1/4 cup baking powder
- 2 Tbsp. salt

Method:
Combine all ingredients in a large bowl. Stir together to blend well. Put in air-tight container. Label. Store in a cool, dry place. Use within 6 to 8 months. Makes about 13 cups of Pancake Mix.

Perfect Pancakes from Mix

from Beatrice Sam, Tofino, B.C.

Makes 10

Ingredients:
- 1 1/2 cups Pancake Mix
- 1 egg slightly beaten
- 1 cup water
- 3 Tbsp. vegetable oil

Method:
Put Pancake Mix in a medium bowl. Combine egg, water and oil in a small bowl. Add egg mixture to Pancake Mix. Add more water for thinner pancakes. Blend well. Let stand 5 minutes. Cook on a hot oiled griddle about 3 to 4 minutes, until browned on both sides. For variety, add your favourite fruit to the batter.

Baking Powder Biscuits

from Margaret Blackstaffe, Victoria, BC

Makes 100 biscuits
Temperature is 400°
Baking time is 15 minutes (approx.)

Ingredients:
- 20 cups flour
- 8 Tbsp. baking powder
- 1 Tsp. salt
- 31/2 cups shortening or margarine
- 1 1/2 qts. milk (approx.)

Method:
Rub or cut fat into dry ingredients until like bread-crumbs. Add milk to make dough not too sticky. Roll 1/4 inch thick. Cut into rounds or squares. Bake on greased pans.

Quick Apple Cake

from Esperanza Kitchen

Serves 30
Temperature is 350°
Baking time is 40 minutes

Ingredients:
- 12 cups chopped apples
- 6 eggs slightly beaten
- 5 cups sugar
- 6 Tsp. cinnamon
- 3 Tsp. nutmeg
- 1 1/2 cups oil
- 6 cups flour
- 3 Tsp. salt
- 3 Tsp. soda

SAUCE:
- 3 cups white sugar
- 3 cups brown sugar
- 3 cups butter
- 3 cups cream

Method:
Add slightly beaten eggs to apples. Then combine sugar, cinnamon, nutmeg, oil, flour, salt and soda. The mixture will be quite dry and hard to stir. Spread in ungreased pan. Bake. Serve with the following SAUCE:
Bring to boil brown and white sugars, butter and cream.

Spanish Rice

from Esperanza Kitchen

Serves 40

Ingredients:
- 16 cups cold water
- 8 cups rice
- 4 pkgs. onion soup mix (2 boxes)
- 4 lbs. hamburger
- 4 - 28 oz. cans tomatoes

Method:
Put in a pot cold water, rice and onion soup mix. Lift with fork occasionally until boiling. Cover and simmer 14 minutes for white rice. 45 minutes for brown rice. Brown hamburger and add to cooked rice. Add canned tomatoes.

Cabbage Rolls

from Esperanza Kitchen

Serves 30
Temperature is 325°
Baking time is 3 hours

Ingredients:
- 5 large cabbage
- 5 lbs. minced beef
- 3/4 cup uncooked rice
- 1 medium onion, grated
- 5 Tbsp. lemon juice
- 10 Tbsp. brown sugar (1/2 cup)
- 5 Tsp. salt
- 1 1/2 Tsp. pepper
- 2 Tsp. paprika
- 10 Tbsp. oil

SAUCE:
- 10 - 8 oz. tins tomato paste
- 2 1/2 cups hot water
- 2 cups brown sugar
- 1 1/4 cups lemon juice
- 1 Tsp. paprika

Method:
Core cabbage. Pour boiling water over them. Let stand 10 min. Combine beef, rice, onion, lemon juice, brown sugar, salt, pepper, paprika. Put spoonfulls of meat mixture on cabbage leaf and roll up. Saute onions in oil. Arrange rolls on top of onions in baking pan. Make sauce by combining sauce ingredients and pour over rolls and onions. Cover and bake.

Chili Con Carne

from Esperanza Kitchen

Serves 40

Ingredients:
- 10 cups red kidney beans
  or
- 2 - 100 oz. tins of kidney beans
- 5 lbs. hamburger
- 10 medium onions
- 1 - 100 oz. can tomatoes
- 10 Tbsp. chili powder
- 1/2 Tsp. pepper
- 15 Tsp. salt

Method:

Cover beans with water and cook for one hour. Brown hamburger and onions together. Add tomatoes and spices. Combine and simmer gently for two hours.

Creole Franks for hungry kids

from Esperanza Kitchen

Serves 40

Ingredients:
- 9 lbs. weiners, sliced
- 1 lb. bacon
- fat
- 3 cups onions, chopped
- 3/4 Tsp. chili powder
- 6 cups unsweetened pineapple
- pineapple juice
- 4 1/2 cups Ketchup
- 3/4 cup green pepper, chopped
- rice

Method:

Fry bacon and drain on paper towel. In some of the fat saute onions, green pepper. Add chili powder, pineapple and some pineapple juice and Ketchup. Add weiners and simmer. Serve with rice.

Sausage Casserole

from Esperanza Kitchen

Serves 40
Temperature is 350°
Baking time is 1 1/2 - 2 hours

Ingredients:
7 large onions, chopped
7 stalks celery, chopped
3 1/2 cups long grain rice, uncooked
5 lb. link sausage
1 - 48 oz. can tomato soup
2 - 14 oz. tins tomato sauce
7 Tsp. brown sugar

Method:
Spread cut up vegetables in baking pan. Layer with rice, suasage, tomato soup and tomato sauce. Dissolve brown sugar into equal amounts of water of the above tins tomato. Pour over all. Cover and cook.

Sloppy Joes

from Margaret Blackstaffe, Victoria, BC

Serves 50-60

Ingredients:
25 lbs. hamburger
10 onions, chopped
5 cups Ketchup
20 Tbsp. brown sugar
20 Tbsp. vinegar
8 Tbsp. prepared mustard
Tomato soup

Method:
Lightly fry onions and hamburger. Combine Ketchup, brown sugar, vinegar and prepared mustard. Add tomato soup till right consistancy. Sloppy as the name implies. Mix all together. Serve over hamburger buns. Good with salad.

Ham Casserole

from Esperanza Kitchen

Serves 30
Temperature is 350°
Baking time is 45 - 60 minutes

Ingredients:

2 2/3 cups onion, chopped
2 2/3 cups green pepper, chopped
10 Tbsp. margarine
5 - 6 cups diced ham
1 1/4 Tsp. dry mustard
5 Tsp. Worcestershire sauce
8 1/2 cups dry minute rice
5 - 19 oz. cans tomatoes
5 - 10 oz. cans cream corn
cheese

Method:

Saute onion and green pepper in margarine. Add ham and brown slightly. Remove from heat and stir in dry mustard and Worcestershire sauce. Place dry minute rice in a buttered casserole. Top with tomatoes and ham mixture. Cover with cream corn. Sprinkle cheese generously on top. Bake.

Chicken Casserole

from Esperanza Kitchen

Serves 40
Slow oven
Baking time is 6 hours

Ingredients:

8 stewing hens
3 Tsp. salt
3 cups flour
10 cups onions, sliced
12 cups carrots, diced
3 cups chicken stock/ Oxo/soup base

Method:

Combine salt, flour and shake the thawed and washed chickens in that mixture. Brown in hot fat. Drain on paper to remove fat. Place in baking pan the onions and carrots. Put chicken on top of vegetables. Pour chicken stock over all and cover pan and bake in slow oven. Six hours if the chicken is tough.

Chinese Chop Suey

from Esperanza Kitchen

Serves 40

Ingredients:

6 lbs. stew meat or round steak
1 1/4 cups oil
6 Tsp. salt
12 medium sized onions, sliced
6 cups sliced mushrooms
6 cups shredded green peppers
6 cups shredded celery
6 cups shredded cabbage
20 cups stock or dissolved bullion cube
6 cans bean sprouts
3/4 cup cornstarch
6 Tbsp. cold water
3/4 cup soy sauce
6 Tbsp. brown sugar

Method:

Cut meat into 1 inch cubes. Heat oil and add salt. Blend. Add onions, green peppers, mushrooms, celery. Saute with meat till meat is lightly browned. Add Chinese cabbage and meat stock. Cover and simmer 45 min. Add bean sprouts. Mix to smooth paste - cornstarch and cold water. Slowly add to meat, stirring constantly till well blended and thick about 5 min. Add soy sauce and brown sugar. Stir until sugar dissolved. Serve with boiled brown rice.

Oven Bar-b-qued Chicken

from Esperanza Kitchen

Serves 40

Ingredients:
10 stewing hens
seasoned flour

Method:
Coat chickens with seasoned flour. Brown on grill in hot fat. Drain on paper towel. Place chicken in casserole.

Bar-b-qued Sauce #1

Probably enough for 40 servings

Ingredients:
7 cups lemon juice
5 cloves finely chopped garlic
1 1/2 cups finely chopped onions
3 1/4 cups vegetable oil
2 Tbsp. salt
2 Tbsp. pepper
2 Tbsp. thyme

Method:
Combine sauce ingredients, cover and refrigerate for one day. Add sauce to chicken parts and bake 4 - 6 hours (2 hours for fryers) in slow oven.

Bar-b-qued Sauce #2

Probably enough for 40 servings

Ingredients:
2 1/4 cups onion
3 Tbsp. margarine
6 Oxo beef cubes
3 cups boiling water
3 cups Ketchup
1 1/2 cups molasses
3/4 cup brown sugar
2 cups vinegar
6 Tsp. dry mustard
1 1/2 Tsp. salt
1 1/2 Tsp. pepper
Dash cayenne

Method:
Place chicken in casserole. Prepare sauce - saute onion in margarine. Add Oxo and boiling water. Add remaining ingredients. Cover and simmer for 20 minutes. Pour sauce over chicken parts and bake in slow oven for 4 - 6 hours (2 hours for fryers) in slow oven.

Bar-b-qued Sauce #3

Probably enough for 20 servings

Ingredients:
- 4 cans frozen concentrated orange juice
- 8 Oxo cubes
- 2 cups boiling water
- 1 cup soy sauce
- 4 Tsp. ground ginger
- 4 cloves garlic carushed or
- 1 Tsp. powdered garlic
- 4 Tsp. salt
- 1 Tsp. pepper

Method:
Combine orange juice, Oxo and boiling water. Add to remaining ingredients and stir well. Pour sauce over chicken parts and bake in slow oven for 4 - 6 hours (2 hours for fryers) in slow oven.

Bar-b-qued Sauce #4

Probably enough for 20 servings

Ingredients:
- 4 cups Ketchup
- 4 Tbsp. Worcestershire sauce
- 4 cups water
- 1 cup vinegar
- 4 Tbsp. brown sugar
- 4 Tsp. salt
- 4 Tsp. celery seed
- 4 Tbsp. instant minced onion

Method:
Combine all ingredients. Pour sauce over chicken parts and bake in slow oven for 4 - 6 hours (2 hours for fryers) in slow oven.

Cheese and Rice Souffle

from Esperanza Kitchen

Serves 30
Temperature is 350°
Baking time is 40 - 60 minutes

Ingredients:

White sauce: 3/4 cup margarine
1 cup + 2 Tbsp. flour
4 1/2 cups milk
12 cups shredded cheese
24 egg yolks, slightly beaten
3 Tsp. salt
1/2 Tsp. pepper
6 cups cooked rice
24 egg whites

Method:

Prepare white sauce by combining margarine, flour and milk. Add cheese. Cook over low heat, stirring constantly until cheese melts. Then add egg yolks, salt/pepper and cooked rice. Remove sauce from heat and pour into large bowl. In a separate bowl beat until stiff but not dry the egg whites. Gently fold whites into cheese mixture. Turn into greased pan. To form crown with spoon make shallow path 1 inch from edges all the way around. Bake. Serve.

Notes

Vegetable Soup

from Esperanza Kitchen

Serves 20

Ingredients:
- 5 small onions, minced
- 10 Tbsp. butter
- 10 qts. meat stock
- 10 cups shredded beets
- 5 cups shredded carrots
- 2 1/2 cups diced celery
- 10 potatoes, diced
- 10 cups shredded cabbage
- 5 cups canned tomatoes
- salt/pepper
- 5 Tbsp. lemon juice or vinegar

Method:
Saute minced onions in butter then add to rest of ingredients. Simmer for about 15 - 20 minutes just until vegetables are tender. Season with lemon juice or vinegar. Serve garnished with sour cream.

Old Fashioned Split Pea Soup

from Esperanza Kitchen

Serves 40

Ingredients:
- 8 cups (4 lbs.)split green/ yellow peas
- 48 cups cold water
- 1 hambone
- 4 cups finely chopped onions
- 4 cups finely diced celery
- 3/4 cup butter or margarine
- 3/4 cup flour

Method:
Pick over and wash split peas. Soak overnight in water. Do not drain. Add hambone but trim off fat, onions and celery. Bring slowly to boiling point. Cover and simmer 3 hours or until peas are tender. Remove ham bone. Cut off any meat, finely dice and return to soup. Skim off fat. Combine margarine and flour. Blend in about 4 cups soup. Stir this mixture into soup and bring to boil, stirring constantly. Season to taste. The hambone gives good flavour.

Clam Chowder

from Esperanza Kitchen

Serves 30

Ingredients:

1 ice cream pail full of
   clams
8 cups cold water
1 lb. salt pork or bacon,
   diced
1 1/4 cups butter or
   margarine
10 medium onions, sliced
3/4 cup flour
1 1/4 Tsp. celery salt
1 1/4 Tsp. pepper
15 cups diced, pared
   potatoes
5 Tsp. salt
clam liquid
15 cups milk (hot pow-
   dered)
3 Tsp. salt
3/4 cup butter or marga-
   rine

Method:

Snip clams quite fine. Place in sauce
pan with water, bring to boil. Drain
reserve liquid. Saute pork, margarine, onions till tender. Add 3/4
cups flour, celery salt and pepper.
Blend. Cook for 8 minutes till tender
and add potatoes, salt and clam
liquid. Then add 15 cups milk (hot,
powdered - otherwise must be
scalded), clams, 3 Tsp. salt and
margarine.

Granola

from Jewell Leighton, Duncan, B.C.

Temperature is 300°
Baking time is about 60 minutes
Uses a Large roasting pan

Ingredients:

4 cups rolled oats
2 cups rolled wheat
1 cup natural coconut
1 cup sunflower seeds
1/2 cup sesame seeds
1/2 cup wheat germ
1/2 cup whole wheat
   flour
1/2 cup corn meal
1/2 cup soya flakes
1 cup chopped nuts
1 cup oil
1/2 cup honey
2 Tbsp. milk

Method:

Heat oil, honey and milk. Stir well.
Add to dry ingredients. Put into
large roasting pan and mix well.
Bake but stir occasionally until oats
and nuts, etc. take on golden roasted
colour. Cool and add dried fruit if
desired (raisins, chopped apricots,
etc.). Makes large batch so can be
halved. The dry ingredients may be
substituted for others of your choice
as long as you maintain the 11 - 12
cup ratio.

Granola

from Hazel Benner, Lennoxville, Quebec

Temperature is 275-325°
Baking time is 20 - 30 minutes
Uses cookie sheets

Ingredients:

5 cups rolled oats
1 cup sesame seeds
1 cup wheat germ or bran
1 cup powdered milk
1 cup vegetable oil
   (not olive oil)
1 cup honey or a bit more
1/2 cup chopped walnuts,
   optional
1 cup coconut
1 cup raisins or currents
1 cup dates, optional
1 Tsp. cinnamon

Method:

Mix dry ingredients except nuts,
coconut and dried fruit. Combine
and warm vegetable oil (you may
substitute 1/3 cup melted margarine) and honey. Mix together and
spread on cookie sheets. Bake in
slow oven until slightly browned.
Add nuts, coconut and fruit during
last ten minutes. Store in air-tight
containers in fridge. Use as cereal or
snacks.

Notes

The Esperanza Story

The quiet waters of the Esperanza Inlet flow between Nootka Island and the west coast of Vancouver Island. The Esperanza community nestles into a steep mountain side on a beautiful bench of land mid way between Tahsis and Zeballos.

During the late 1930's, loggers, miners, fishermen and Nootka speaking Indians heavily populated this remote and rugged coast line.

There were no medical facilites or doctors for 200 mile between Port Alberni and Port Alice.

In 1937, pioneer Shantyman missionary Percy E. Wills and Dr. Herman McLean set sail from Victoria to assess the medical needs of the area. The further they sailed, the more human pain and suffering they encountered. They became convinced that they must begin at once to build a hospital.

The missionary and the Doctor soon identified a sheltered building site with a sparkling fresh water mountain stream. Without delay, the two men put their axes to the forest, clearing an area for the first buildings. On November 1, 1937, the first emergency surgery was performed at the Esperanza General Hospital.

Dr. McLean's wife, Marion, their five children and two nurses soon came to Esperanza to join the Doctor.

The hospital and the support community grew to meet the need of area residents over the next thirty-seven years. Hundreds of babies were delivered, as many surgeries were performed and countless medical problems treated.

The Doctor's missionary heart was as concerned for the emotional needs of his patients as for their physical needs. Many left Esperanza with renewed physical health and a fresh new hope for the future.

Today; the Esperanza community with fifteen homes and build-ings, beautifully kept gardens, marine fuel station and coffee shop continues as a missionary outpost.

For a complete history of Esperanza, watch for the inspiring book "Not Without Hope" by Louise Johnson.

INDEX

INDEX

INDEX

ORDER FORM

If you would like to order additional copies of *The Esperanza Cook Book*, please send $10.00 plus $2.00 postage & handling to:

Louise Johnson
Box 411
Tofino, B.C., V0R 2Z0

or

Maple Lane Publishing
34968 Sim Road
Matsuqi, B.C. V0X 1S0